To my spiritual mother, Joyce Meyer

Now to him who is able to do far more
abundantly beyond all that we ask or think,
according to the power that works within us.
EPHESIANS 3:20 (ESV)

CONTENTS

AN INVITATION TO THE UNEXPECTED

To expect the unexpected shows a thoroughly modern intellect.

—OSCAR WILDE

For my fiftieth birthday, Nick gave me the greatest gift ever. He invited 150 of our dearest friends to a huge celebration he'd planned for a year. It was a dinner cruise with wonderful food, dancing, a beautiful cake, and lots of laughs.

It was one of the most amazing nights of my life. And, as I'd find out later that evening, it would also become one of the saddest nights of my life.

While I was on the boat dancing Zorba the Greek with all my friends, I missed multiple phone calls from my brother Andrew. I discovered them on the drive home, along with an unexpected text: "Mum is gone."

In a matter of minutes, I went from soaking in the memories of the happiest night imaginable to feeling utterly heartbroken. I was whiplashed by the shock of it all.

I had just spoken with my mother earlier in the day, when my other brother, George, had helped her FaceTime with me. Although she had been ill for some time, I thought we had at least a few more months. I had even told her I would call after the party, as I expected to give her a full report on all the fun.

I'll always cherish the last memory I have of her—looking at her face, seeing her sweet smile, and hearing her say, "I love you."

Such an unexpected gift right before an unexpected loss.

It's strange how life can be that way—so full of surprises, both good and bad, and sometimes all in the same day. We can go from cleaning up after a birthday party to planning a funeral. From hearing a shocking diagnosis to welcoming our first grandchild. From a layoff notice at lunch to a marriage proposal at dinner. From an unexpected car repair one day to a raise and promotion the next. From planning a vacation to losing everything in a hurricane.

It seems the unexpected is one of the mysteries of life—something we have no control over but are guaranteed to experience every single day.

Of course, we don't usually mind the unexpected when it's happy or inconsequential. But when the unexpected strikes fear in our hearts or is deeply painful—like losing someone we cherish—it can throw us into such a devastated state that we withdraw or shut down, unable to move forward in . . .

- Our marriage
- A friendship
- Our health
- Our career
- Our faith

Whiplashed and then immobilized by something we never expected, we end up stuck in a place we never wanted to be. Stuck in a place where our world shrinks and we hide inside of it, living a story far smaller than God intends. Forfeiting the future that could have been. The destiny we were born to live.

We've all been there, tempted to pull back and hide when we were wounded, disappointed, or disillusioned. When we faced failure or endured another heartache. When we suffered a loss that was more than we felt we could bear. When we made promises to ourselves that we'd never let such pain happen to us again. But we can't keep those kinds of promises. Not if we want to step into all of *God's* promises. Not if we want to live with all the passion he placed inside of us. Not if we want to fulfill the purpose and destiny he has for us.

No.

We cannot shrink back in fear and go forward in faith at the same time. We cannot settle for our *less* and pursue his *more* at the same time. It's just not possible.

What *is* possible is accepting his gracious invitation to trust him more in the face of our pain. To move into a deeper intimacy with him and let him heal our hearts. To develop relentless faith so that the next time life throws us a curve ball—which life most certainly will—we are able to bat it out of the park and still live the adventure he's planned for us. And maybe we'll even live a version of the adventure that's beyond what we could ever have hoped or imagined—all because of the unexpected that interrupted our lives in the first place.

I believe with all my heart that it's possible for every Christian to learn how to live with a faith so confident in God, it can't be shaken—even when the ground underneath is giving way. That's what Abraham did. God extended to him the same invitation he extends to us—to trust with all his heart—and Abraham said yes, even though he had no idea where his yes would lead. He willingly stepped into the unexpected without knowing where he was going, who he would meet, or what it might cost. He didn't know any of the pain that might lie ahead, but he knew God would be with him. He knew God would guide him, protect him, and provide for him—and he refused to be shaken:

> By faith Abraham, when called to go to a place he would later receive as his inheritance, obeyed and went, *even though he did not know where he was going.*
>   HEBREWS 11:8, emphasis added

Like Abraham, I know what it feels like to go forth not knowing where I'm going. To risk it all and trust God with an unknown future. Through the years of my Christian walk, I've gone from volunteering in a local youth ministry in my early twenties, to running a global anti-trafficking organization in twelve nations, to continuing to launch new initiatives into my fifties. I've gone from living in Australia where I started in ministry, married, and had children, to moving our ministry base to the United States. I have repeatedly stepped into unexpected places, only to find myself accomplishing unexpected ventures, and seeing God turn up in the most unexpected ways—all because I said yes every single time, even when I didn't have any idea where it would lead.

Since I surrendered my life fully to Jesus, he's been teaching me unshakeable faith. Relentless faith. Unwavering faith. Teaching me to trust him more every time he asks. Teaching me to embrace the unexpected. He's been cultivating in me the same kind of faith that propelled Abraham further into his destiny as the father of Isaac, and ultimately the father of many nations. The same kind of faith that led Abraham to trust God more, even in the face of sheer hopelessness:

Against all hope, Abraham in hope believed and so became the father of many nations, just as it had been said to him, "So shall your offspring be." Without weakening in his faith, he faced the fact that his body was as good as dead—since he was about a hundred years old—and that Sarah's womb was also dead. Yet he did not waver through unbelief regarding the promise of God, but was strengthened in his faith and gave glory to God, being fully persuaded that God had power to do what he had promised.

ROMANS 4:18–21

When God gave Abraham such an outlandish and unexpected promise, he simply believed God's promise—he risked hope against all rational hope. He didn't deny the facts of his circumstances, but he refused to believe they were the whole truth because they did not account for God's promise. He did not waver or doubt, and because of that, his faith grew even stronger. When, at last, Isaac was born, Abraham gave all the glory to God.

Imagine the difference we could make if we learned to face the unexpected in our lives as Abraham did. If we learned to do the unexpected while facing the unexpected. What if we belicved instead of feared in the face of the unknown? What if we courageously moved through loss and disappointment, believing God has purpose for it on the other side? What if we got up every day believing God for the best, knowing we might possibly encounter the worst?

I believe we can live this expectantly—this hopefully, this freely, this faith-filled—in the face of *everything* that comes our way. Even the unexpected.

13

When I planned this book, I didn't realize how timely it would be. How on point it would be for all we're grappling with in the world today. From the day I reviewed the outline with our publisher until the day it went to press, the news reports have been filled with the unexpected, with shocking events that are hard to understand and can sometimes shake our faith:

- An active shooter at a school, church, or concert
- A car racing down a sidewalk intentionally targeting pedestrians—not just in one city, but in multiple cities
- History-making hurricanes devastating millions of lives
- A demonstration intended to unite that only divides
- Another suicide bomber in a crowded market or arena
- A government leader's disappointing choices
- The passing of laws contradicting our values or beliefs
- A UNESCO World Heritage site left in ruins
- Another genocide

Some days these events seem so far away, and other days they hit way too close to home. In all these situations, God wants us to be faith-filled believers shining the light of Christ in a dark world. He wants us to learn how to walk with confidence through every unexpected challenge life throws our way—not only so we can be a powerful testimony to others, but also so we can develop a more intimate relationship with him ourselves.

When we went back to Australia for my mum's funeral, I stood at her graveside service watching her casket being lowered into the ground, and all I could think was, *I'm next.* It wasn't a depressing or morbid thought. It was just a realization of the natural order of life. Typically, you first bury your grandparents, then your parents, and then, you're the next generation to go. That thought stayed with me for days, and it made me more determined than ever to make my life count. To be sure I was doing all that God had called me to do. To lead as many souls to Jesus as I possibly can. It made me resolute in my commitment to Christ, to walk by faith, and to embrace the unexpected. Even during the season of writing this book, God challenged me again, inviting me to let him heal a wound so deep I didn't know it was there.

Through that tender story, other stories from my life, as well as those of dear friends, I'll share what I've learned about how to walk by faith in hopes that you might better understand how fear attacks and how you can overcome its debilitating effects—no matter how heartbreaking the unexpected is. Whether . . .

- A life-threatening diagnosis
- A cutting relational wound
- Deepening disappointment
- A tidal wave of relentless losses
- A purposeless season of life
- A hidden hurt yet to be healed

On the pages ahead, I can't wait to introduce you to my friends, Adrian and Jayne, Amanda and LoriAnn, Kylie and Laura. They are ordinary people doing extraordinary things because, when faced with the unexpected, they accepted God's invitation to trust him more and walk in greater faith. They are real people who were willing to be vulnerable, to let me share their stories, to help you to keep moving forward—from where you are to where God wants you to go.

Unexpected

I have no doubt this book is in your hands because God has a life of adventure planned for you. I know he created you on purpose, for a purpose—and he never wants fear *of* the unexpected or *from* the unexpected to hold you back. So, as you read this book, as you allow the Holy Spirit to light your path, let's go together. Let's leave fear behind, move forward in faith, and embrace the adventure of the unexpected.

Love,
Christine

Chapter One

WHEN THE UNEXPECTED INTERRUPTS

Living Expectantly

True stability results when presumed order and presumed
disorder are balanced. A truly stable system expects the
unexpected, is prepared to be disrupted, waits to be transformed.

TOM ROBBINS

"Chris, you have cancer."

Not quite the words I was expecting to hear as I was unpacking, having arrived in Sydney just two hours earlier. Nick and I, along with our girls, Catherine and Sophia, were in town to attend the annual weeklong worship conference at Hillsong Church—always the highlight of our year, where we came to be refreshed and receive direction from God. It was my twenty-fifth year to attend, and I felt such a sense of expectancy. I knew God had something significant for me.

We had flown fourteen hours from LA where we had moved five years before in order to expand the work of A21, our global anti-trafficking organization. We loved living in the US, *and* we loved coming home.

As I listened to my doctor calling from the US, time seemed to stand still, as though it was giving my mind a chance to catch up to what I was hearing. I looked out the window past the boats sailing in Darling Harbour and focused on the Anzac Bridge. So much had happened in a week's time.

Just the Wednesday before, I had been in Dallas filming a live TV special about overcoming the pain of the past and moving into one's future. I love seeing people set free from the bondage and strongholds that keep them enslaved to the pain of their past. I've never lost touch with how Jesus set me free, and I have spent three decades helping others find that same freedom. God had always been faithful to use his Word to heal before, and he had been faithful again. I was blessed to hear about the number of people who responded to the teaching, calling in for prayer and support that night after the show.

Saying goodbye to the crew and thanking them for their part in so many lives being touched, I noticed that my throat was sore and that I sounded hoarse—but I didn't think too much about it as I headed to my hotel. After all, I had talked all day. And most of the evening. I talk for a living. I talk for pleasure. I talk to sort things out in my head. I'm Greek—and a woman. Talking is part of my DNA. In short, I never stop talking. So I logically chalked up my sore throat to that day's enthusiasm and looked forward to a good night's sleep.

But when I woke up Thursday morning, I could barely lift my head off the pillow. My head hurt so badly and I was so sick—something I rarely experience. As I became more awake, I knew that this wasn't normal. I could feel something hanging down the back of my throat on the left side. I could feel a tiny lump on the right. And I had this uneasy feeling that something was wrong, very wrong.

I called Nick, who was on the other side of the world in Madagascar on a mission trip, to tell him my concerns. After listening to me describe my symptoms, he prayed for me and reassured me that it would all be okay and that he'd be home in just a few days. Then, I headed back to LA to speak at a church's women's conference and their weekend services.

GOD WAS WITH ME

I know the grace of God carried me through Saturday and Sunday as I'd never felt that ill in all my years of ministry. When Nick got home on Sunday afternoon, I was so relieved. I knew I needed to see a doctor, but because I'd never needed one in the five years that I'd lived in the States, we didn't know who to call. As evening approached, we discussed our options: waiting to see my physician in Australia, since we were heading there the next week, or going to an urgent care center that night. We decided first to go for a walk to talk further and pray. We needed clear direction.

Despite my uneasiness and how I felt, I could sense that God was with me. Walking in the park, we crossed paths with a dear friend. As we stopped to say hello, we began talking, and I shared what I was experiencing. He highly recommended his doctor whose office was close by, and since Nick and I had been asking God for direction, we believed this was his answer. We contacted the doctor, and surprisingly, she agreed to see me the next morning—even though she wasn't taking new clients and had a packed schedule. God was taking care of me, and I knew it.

As soon as the doctor examined me, she ordered blood work, referred me to an ENT, and scheduled a series of tests—all fast-tracked within the next three days since I had to leave for Sydney Wednesday night. When I met with the ENT, he was greatly concerned about the nodules that had formed on my vocal cords. He felt they were so serious that he explicitly told me to speak very little in the coming weeks. "Minimally," he had said, and then he added, "and whatever you do, don't sing."

He had no idea that I was headed to the annual Hillsong Worship Conference. I nodded my head, because I knew he was giving me sound medical counsel, but deep inside, I found it all so humorous and surreal. Imagine the most talkative woman you know being told not to talk or sing while attending a worship conference. *Are you kidding me?*

So yes, I had been expecting the call from my doctor, but I wasn't expecting her to say cancer—a word that had the power to trigger so many painful memories.

THE SAME NEWS, THE SAME CITY

The C Word.

We've all known someone.

I knew someone. He was the first man I had ever loved. I was just eighteen when my mum told me, "Christina, your father has cancer." She had said it just as honestly and bluntly then as my doctor was saying it now. I didn't want to believe it about him then, just like I didn't want to believe it about me now. The emotions of my past were compounding those of my present, and though I didn't want to relive what I had been through thirty years before, I couldn't stop the flashbacks.

I had witnessed firsthand how cancer—not to mention chemo and radiation therapy—consumes a healthy body.

I watched my dad go from a strong, independent man to a weak, frail one. I watched his beautiful, thick black hair fall out of his head. I watched his strong frame slowly diminish to skin and bones. When he could no longer drive, I drove him to his appointments. I sat in waiting rooms while he was in surgery.

I learned what a financial burden endless treatments can be.

And I experienced the suffocating effect of fear. I saw my mother feel helpless, hopeless, afraid, and lost. I prayed desperate, fervent prayers that seemed to change nothing. I felt fear like never before as it gradually took up residence in our home and in our hearts. I had faith and hope that my dad would be healed. But I heard him being sick, ever so sick, always sick. And I saw what stalled hope could do to a family as our hearts sank low.

When we finally heard his doctor use the word *remission*, we thought we were in the clear. We were elated. It had been such a long time since we had any expectation of normal.

But then, just two weeks later, the unexpected happened. Again.

I raced home from work when Mum sent for me. The ambulance was parked outside our house, and a crowd of neighbors had gathered on our lawn. I walked in the front door to see my mum holding my dad's head in her lap. She had been helping him put on his shirt.

I've never been able to un-see that moment.

I've never been able to un-feel that shock and heartbreak.

I loved my dad dearly.

The grief that unfolded in the following months was devastating. I saw my distraught brothers try to process life without their hero. I saw my mum, who was normally a pillar of strength, become almost nonfunctional. She and my dad deeply loved each other, and I don't think she ever imagined life without him.

Everything changed when my dad died—including me. His death triggered a downward spiral in my life that I didn't know how to stop, because when you don't know how to process grief, you try to numb it. You will do anything, absolutely anything, to not *feel*—the loss, the pain, the heartache.

Life without my father has never stopped aching me.

He wasn't there to watch me walk across the stage and receive my college degree.

He didn't get to meet Nick.

He couldn't walk me down the aisle on my wedding day.

My daughters won't ever meet their grandfather.

I've never been able to call him and tell him that we rescued another girl through the work of A21.

I've never been able to hand him one of my books.

He's never heard me teach.

All because of cancer.

So, yes, I was very familiar with the word *cancer*—and with the fear and pain that it injects into the life of a family.

And now the doctor was speaking that word, not about an acquaintance, a friend, or someone on television, but about *me*. Me. A healthy, fit wife and mother of two beautiful girls. I was hearing the same news in the same city where I'd lived through it decades before, and buried my dad because of it.

Still staring at the bridge, I stopped recalling long enough to hear my doctor explain: "You actually have four separate conditions in that area: a growth on the left side of your throat, nodules on your vocal cords, a throat infection, and thyroid cancer."

SO UNEXPECTED

As I stood there trying to comprehend all that the doctor was saying, my heart wrenched as I thought of Nick and the girls. *What would this mean for our lives? Was the cancer isolated? Had it spread?*

I knew I wouldn't live forever—not here on earth—but this was so . . . unexpected.

And yet, if we stop to think about it, every day is filled with the unexpected, with the unanticipated. We make our to-do lists. We set out thinking our day will go according to plan. But it doesn't, because interruptions that we never saw coming invade our lives and usher in the unexpected. Some of those interruptions are small and harmless, like running into an old friend at lunch. And some are big and inconvenient, like having a flight canceled or rerouted. Some of them are happy, like receiving a surprise marriage proposal or a promotion. And some of them are heartbreaking, like getting a call that a dear friend has died or learning our spouse is having an affair. And some of them, some of them are just plain shocking, like when your doctor says, "Chris, you have cancer."

But as surprising as the unexpected is, we need to remember that our unexpected is never unexpected to God. God knew this day would come in my life, and he was already in this day waiting for me. Fear was trying to grip me like it naturally does when we receive any bad news, but I knew I couldn't let it overwhelm me.

And yet, I couldn't stop thinking about Nick and the girls. I didn't want my daughters to go through what I had gone through with my dad, and I didn't want them to grow up without a mother. *What about all the dreams Nick and I had for the future? What about the ministry and our team?*

I knew I had to stop my mind from going too far. I knew enough to recognize this train of thought could speed quickly down its track and derail me into a dark place. I knew that I needed to be in faith—for all our sakes. Like many situations I'd been through before, I knew there was a choice that was still mine to make: *Would I walk in fear or faith?*

It was faith that had always propelled me forward through my circumstances in the past, so I chose faith in my present situation. That didn't mean, however, that the fear went away. It still tempted me, but I knew that being tempted with fear wasn't the same as giving into it—and not giving into it was the only way I could overcome its grip. So, even while I was processing so many thoughts in my head—about my dad, about Nick and the girls, about cancer, about the ministry and my future—in my heart I was falling into the arms of my heavenly Father. Deep down, I knew that I trusted God.

Time and time again, in big things and in small ones, I had learned to run *to* God and not *from* him. I had learned that whatever my situation, he was there with me. I had taken it to heart that God is good. God does good. God works all things together for my good,[1] and that *all things* really includes *all* things, even bad things that happen to good people, like what was happening to me now.

Cancer was definitely bad; certainly not good. Certainly not from God. I do not believe that God sends sickness, because there is no sickness in heaven or in God himself. The Word promises us that God gives us good and perfect gifts, because he is good—and no kind of cancer is a good or perfect gift.[2] Cancer, like all sickness, is a part of the curse. Because we live in a fallen world, bad things do happen to good people.

So, I had to find the strength to fight this fight of faith.[3]

I had no desire to go straight home. I wanted to stay at the conference for the week to be in a faith-filled environment and to sing. It was going to be a week filled with praise and worship and the teaching of the Word of God, and I wanted to build myself up spiritually for what might be ahead medically.

"Leslie," I began as I found my voice, "it's okay. Cancer is not terminal. Life is terminal. I will live every second of every day that God has ordained for me to live on this earth, and then I will go home. The devil has no authority over my life. The blood of Jesus covers me, and he will take me home when he wants me."

I could hear my voice growing stronger. I could feel my faith taking over. I could feel courage swelling higher. Only God could have given me such strength in that moment.

"I don't know how I'm going home, but like most people, I imagine that death will be the doorway. I just don't think it's time yet. I'm not afraid of dying. That is inevitable, and I just refuse to allow the word *cancer* to grip me with fear."

I'm sure all of that sounded strange to my doctor—especially since I'd only known her for four days. But I had to speak from my heart what I knew to be the truth—for my sake—whether it made sense to anyone else or not. I wasn't denying reality, just its power to control me.

I knew that I couldn't control the unexpected any more than I could stop an earthquake, tsunami, or hurricane. I had to say it because I believe in the goodness of God, even when I could feel fear trying to grip me. I knew there would be a journey ahead—whether short or long. Either way, I had to stay anchored to Jesus—the one in whom my hope relied, the one who held my future. I had to keep my faith alive. And I couldn't let the memories of the past get entangled with my present.

"Tell me what we need to do," I continued. "If I need to come home straight away, I will, but I am at a conference this week that is themed, 'No Other Name,' and I believe that there is a name that is higher than the name of cancer, and that is the name of Jesus. We are on a battlefield, not a playground. It's time to go to war. You tell me what to do medically, and I will fight this spiritually, and whatever happens, Jesus will have the final victory."

FEEDING FAITH, STARVING FEAR

Based on my doctor's advice, I stayed. And against the ENT's advice, I sang, but not out of foolishness. I just knew in my heart that I had to make God bigger in my mind than the news about cancer. I wanted to magnify him and lift him up. I knew that I had to put all my heart into the praise and worship, because it was as critical to my healing as anything the doctors might require in the coming weeks.

I knew I was in a battle and that the enemy never plays fair. He had come for my voice, to silence me—now and forever. But I had been through enough challenges throughout my life to understand that if I did some of the expected things in the unexpected moments—like put into practice biblical principles I had learned thus far in life—I could expect a better outcome. And I could keep the fear away.

So I did. I sang and praised and worshiped Jesus all week, and at the end of the week, I returned home to the States ready to face what lie ahead.

I also called on a few faithful and faith-filled friends whom I could trust to pray for me—friends I knew in the coming weeks would speak faith to me when I might not be strong enough to stand alone in the face of the fear. We're all human, and we all need prayer warriors who will be there when we need them.

I didn't share my condition with anyone else, because I've learned that if you talk to too many people, someone will inevitably want to tell you about their favorite aunt who died of the same kind of cancer you have. For some reason, people think those kinds of stories bless you. But for my faith to thrive, I knew I had to keep myself encamped in what I have come to call a "faith cocoon." It's when I proactively decide to stay diligent in the Word, listen continuously to worship music, and allow only faith-filled voices to speak into my life about a particular situation. So, at the moment, it was critical whom I trusted to fight this battle alongside me.

I stayed in the Word and found key verses to pray and believe—promises for healing, for a future. I kept them on my phone so I could read them throughout the day. I read them aloud, committed to speaking only the Word. There were times when I remembered hearing all the fear my mum had spoken when my dad was sick. She was gripped with fear the entire time as it was all she knew. But I had grown up in Christ since then, and knew to speak only faith. I had learned that we either feed fear or we feed faith, and that I had the power to choose which one I would feed. So, I fed my faith.

I worked at keeping out all negativity, which included resisting the temptation to go online and research all that I could about the kind of cancer I was facing. I knew that wouldn't build my faith but only tempt me with more to worry over and be fearful about. I already knew the negative side of cancer. I had lived through it all with my dad, so I didn't need to read about any of the possibilities.

And, I believed God for a miracle. I wanted to be delivered *from* this situation. I believed that God could supernaturally heal me and simply make the cancer disappear from my body. He had done it for others, and I desperately wanted him to do it for me. But I soon discovered that God was not going to supernaturally deliver me *from* this. He was going to walk me *through* it.

TIME TO GO *THROUGH*

Whether we ever understand *why*, the only way to overcome any unexpected shock is *through*. No matter how much we wish we could go around a situation, under it, over it, or be delivered from it, there are times God wants to walk us through a process, because that is what's best for us.

The challenge then becomes choosing not to allow the enemy to use these unplanned and upsetting events to rob us of life. The enemy wants to derail our lives from the plans and purposes of God—if not for a lifetime, then at least for a season. He wants to pull our focus away from God's promises and divert it to our crisis. He wants to paralyze us in the present and to veil our vision and hope for our future.

But I have found that moving *through* whatever you're facing isn't about merely surviving until it's over, and then numbing your way through the rest of your life. Moving *through* is about continuing to live a life of purpose and passion—of always moving forward, never losing sight of your objective—no matter how devastating the unexpected is. Facing cancer renewed my resolve: *While I know that I will live forever in eternity, I choose to live fully alive here on earth and make every second count for God and his kingdom purposes until the day I die.*

I was still a mother to my children, so I was not going to let the news of cancer bench me from parenting my girls. I was still a wife to Nick, and I would not allow this news to take me away mentally and emotionally. I wanted to be present in every moment. I still wanted to keep leading our ministry and make every one of my days on the planet count for the glory of God.

Cancer was a condition I had, not who I was. I didn't want one unexpected condition to define my overall condition, so I was not going to let it set the tone of my home, derail my faith, or stop me from living in every moment God had for me. I couldn't. But that decision was an hourly—and sometimes moment-to-moment—fight in my mind and will to stay on point. Regardless of what I was going *through*, I was still a child of God, a mother, a wife, a teacher, a friend, and a daughter—and I had to fight to stay focused.

My diagnosis came during one of the busiest and biggest seasons of my ministry year, and I had no margin to do all this, but battles never come at a convenient time.

I WILL NEVER BE THE SAME

The rest of July became a series of tests, ultrasounds, and more tests and more ultrasounds. I sat in many waiting rooms full of cancer patients. So many of those patients sat all alone, and I could see the fear in their eyes. People who had lost all their hair. People who could no longer walk unaided. People marked with radiation lines. People bruised from endless needles and bumps. My heart almost stopped as I watched a father wheel his son into the treatment room. I have two daughters who have never been sick. Not like this. Dear God. Mercy. Grace.

My heart broke for them. Compassion overwhelmed me, and I knew why I was there. An unexpected illness had led me to an unexpected place, and I needed to see this. I needed to feel this. "Though I walk *through* the valley of the shadow of death . . . Your rod and Your staff, they comfort me" (Psalm 23:4 NKJV, emphasis added). Though I had learned that my condition was comparatively mild, and the type of cancer I had was highly curable through surgery, I had to walk through my own valley. Yet for many people I met, their path seemed so much harder and darker. In my case, cancer was isolated. Contained. Curable. For many of these people, cancer was running rampant throughout their bodies.

God, why?

There are so many questions I will never have the answers to this side of eternity, *but I could do what I could do and leave God to do what only he could do.* I needed to seize this opportunity to bring light, life, hope, and joy into the midst of darkness and despondency, so I had powerful conversations with patients and doctors alike, and actually began to look forward to my appointments. God was doing something in me, and Jesus was in those waiting rooms with those people because his Spirit lives in me. I was there, so he was there. Would I be bold enough to reach out, touch, love, and pray for these people? Could I believe God for those who no longer could believe for themselves?

Yes. Some of my most precious ministry moments happened in those waiting rooms and hospitals—where I met people unexpectedly and had unexpected opportunities to share the gospel and speak hope. Because of that, I will never be the same.

Many of us want a platform ministry when there are already abundant ministry opportunities available to us in waiting rooms all over the world. How many are waiting for us to go to them while we are waiting for them to come to us?

People are waiting for us everywhere. In the cubicle next to ours at work. In the checkout line at the supermarket. In the seat next to us in class. In the chair next to ours at the salon. On the subway ride home. On the sidelines of the soccer game. At the close of a deal. They are waiting.

When they ran a second test on my larynx to check the nodules, the ENT gave me the report personally. "I don't know what happened, but the nodules are gone." There was no need for surgery.

He had told me to speak very little. He had told me not to sing. But I did, and I received a miracle—and that miracle became an encouraging anchor for my soul. Why I received a miracle only for my nodules and not my thyroid or throat, I don't know, but I kept trusting God.

Two weeks after receiving that phone call from Leslie, telling me that I had cancer, I had the growth in my throat removed during a one-hour surgery. It was a delicate procedure. The surgeon had to go in between my larynx and my trachea—so close to the proximity of my voice box, so close to affecting the instrument God had given me to speak faith and healing and hope to the world. What if I woke up and couldn't speak anymore? I prayed fervently for the surgeon and put my faith in God.

When the pathology report came back all clear, it was a great relief to all of us, as that was the greatest concern of all my conditions. If it had been cancerous, it would have had a worse potential than the cancer on my thyroid.

And while I was so thankful, I was uncomfortably aware that someone else, perhaps one of those I sat with in one of those waiting rooms, would be getting a very different report that very same day. I prayed that God would give that person grace.

In September, I had a thyroidectomy, which removed half of my thyroid, and there is no trace of cancer in my body to this day. I still go for checkups. At first, they were once every two months, then four months, then six months, now once a year. I get a yearly reminder of my mortality and that life is a gift.

I am so grateful.

That my life was interrupted.

By the unexpected.

UNEXPECTED IS NEVER WASTED

I don't ever again want to go through what I did. I don't ever again want to hear those words, "Chris, you have cancer." While sitting in those waiting rooms with my dad was hard, sitting there when I was the patient was worse. Especially, when I looked at the mothers caring for their sick children.

But I'm thankful that because of the unexpected, who I am today is different from the Christine I was a few years ago. I'm much more compassionate, much more empathetic to people's pain, much more understanding when people go through a challenge. I do wish it hadn't happened, but I wouldn't want to go back to who I was before it happened.

I believe it's time for us to get good at navigating the unexpected, to embrace and understand that through unexpected occurrences in life—both good and bad—we need to trust God, anticipating him to move in it while he moves us through it. We need to realize that he never expected us to live boring and predictable lives, even though we work hard to create regular routines. He's called us to live lives full of joys and sorrows, battles and celebrations, successes and failures, ups and downs. And he wants us to learn how to live expecting to gain from the unexpected, especially as the world grows ever more chaotic and unpredictable.

I travel all over the globe, and I see firsthand how our world is changing. Whether I'm in airports with tighter and tighter security, or walking the streets of Thailand where child trafficking is off the charts, I see how we need to trust God with the future. Terrorism—something we never talked about decades ago—seems to be running rampant and getting closer to home. There is economic, political, social, moral, and environmental instability on every continent. Uncertainty surrounds us regardless of where we live. And no matter what kind of bubble we try to construct to manage our safety and security—physically, financially, or spiritually—trials and tribulations are going to come just as Jesus warned us.[4] And, in our humanness, we will try to control everything—including God. Yet, we serve a God who refuses to be controlled by us. That's because part of the mystery and the adventure of following Jesus is to trust him no matter what is going on around us. To keep our hearts completely open to him, so that when the unexpected happens, he can use it for our good. To free him to use the unexpected, a necessary catalyst, to grow us, sanctify us, and help us see life with a whole new perspective, because nothing grows without disruption and interruption—without the unexpected.

If we could get this truth deeply woven into the fabric of our being, we would be far less fearful in a world that is complex and ever-changing. We could relax in knowing that while we cannot expect to control the unexpected, God is in control of everything, and therefore we can expect that he will be faithful to the promises he has given us in his Word.

- We can expect that his grace will be sufficient for us (2 Corinthians 12:9).
- We can expect that he will never leave us nor forsake us (Hebrews 13:5).
- We can expect that he is working all things together for our good and his glory (Romans 8:28).
- We can expect that no weapon forged against us will prevail (Isaiah 54:17).
- We can expect to be more than conquerors through Christ Jesus who strengthens us (Romans 8:37).
- We can expect that greater is he that is in us than he who is in the world (1 John 4:4).
- We can expect our God to be for us (Romans 8:31).
- We can expect God to be our very present help in trouble (Psalm 46:1).
- We can expect God to care for us (1 Peter 5:7).
- We can expect Jesus Christ to be consistent (Hebrews 13:8).
- We can expect streams in our desert (Isaiah 43:19).
- We can expect impenetrable walls to come down (Joshua 6:20).
- We can expect God to make a way where there is no way (Isaiah 43:16).
- We can expect our mourning to turn to gladness (Psalm 30:11).
- We can expect our sorrow to be turned to joy (Psalm 30:11).
- We can expect our broken heart to be bound up (Psalm 147:3).

- We can expect deliverance from our enemies (Psalm 60:12).
- We can expect our giants to be defeated (1 Samuel 14:47).
- We can expect that no temptation will be more than we can bear (1 Corinthians 10:13).
- We can expect that he who promised will be faithful (Hebrews 10:23).

God wants us to learn how to accept every unexpected event as an invitation to trust Jesus and his Word, to expect his goodness all the way through. A life lived like that is one of the most powerful forces on the planet—because there's a momentum of courage and faith that propels us into new places.

What if we learned to embrace the unpredicted shocks, stressors, and uncertainties in life and then use them for our gain? Maybe there's a perspective, an ingredient, in the way we process life that needs to change. Maybe there's a level of trust even higher than to believe that "for those who love God all things work together for good" (Romans 8:28 ESV). Maybe there's more.

I still want to cling to Romans 8:28, and watch God unfold all the good that he's planned for my life. But I also want to cling to the *even-more* perspective that he has for us. That is the process I want us to walk through together in this book. I want you to raise your sights to a new level of faith and trust in the God who strengthens you to remain unflinching, unshakeable, immoveable in the face of any unexpected events. I want your faith and trust in God to be so focused that you live each day anticipating the good he wants to do for you. I want peace to rule and reign in all the places of your heart, instead of worry, anxiety, and stress.[5] I want your mind and your body to relax in confident trust, for God's endless joy to fill you over and over again, so that nothing really knocks you off your feet ever. I want you to live in expectation of your future every day.

I believe you can get there.

And I can show you how.

But first, we have to uproot any fear that has established itself in our hearts. The kind that has taken up residence in our emotions and conditioned our responses—anxiety, panic, stress, dread, nervousness, withdrawal. We're all tempted with these feelings. We all go through unexpected events that make these kinds of reactions completely understandable. But the truth is that God doesn't intend for us to live mastered by them. He intends for us to master them instead.

Nick and I have dear friends, Adrian and Jayne, who went through an experience with their infant son that no parent ever wants to face. Their story, which I share in the next chapter, is a journey of choosing faith over fear on a daily basis, and it is full of understanding that can show us how to live free from the grip of fear, help us walk in greater faith, and embrace every unexpected adventure in our future.

Chapter Two

WHEN THE UNEXPECTED BRINGS FEAR

Moving Forward in Faith

The unexpected is usually what brings the unbelievable.
—MANDY KELLOGG RYE

Adrian reached down and touched Fraser's emaciated body. The sun was reaching through the blinds and stretching across Fraser's bloated stomach. Staring blankly at the tubes and monitor wires, Adrian faithfully thanked God for his precious son. For one more day.

The previous night had been one more night of darkness and quiet, violently interrupted by sadness and exhausted sobbing. The kind of sobbing that releases more than just grief. More than just pent-up pain. The kind like an imploding building that can't be stopped from falling in on itself.

Another child in the hospital ward had died. Another family had collapsed in sorrow.

Children are a gift. Children aren't supposed to die.

The ward had nine when Fraser was admitted, and now there were only six.

God, you have to fight for us. I don't know if I have any fight left in me. I'm trusting you to make a way for us to get through this.

Even though morning brought relief, Adrian knew Jayne and the kids would arrive soon. He knew the kids would see the empty bed right away.

I don't want to explain heaven again. I don't want them to see all this anymore.

Their questions were always the same. "Will Fraser go there too? If he does, will we see him again? We will, right?"

Josh, being the oldest at seven, seemed to comprehend the most. He was the one who had prayed for a brother—and at one time had asked why God would have given them a sick brother. It was a painful moment for Jayne, but she had answered him carefully. "Well, would you love him any more if he were well?"

"No."

"I think God looks down and he isn't shocked by any of this," Jayne continued, attempting to nurture Josh's perspective through her own pain. "I think he believes in us to be a family who will love Fraser for as long as we have him and love each other through this. He trusts us."

It seemed Adrian and Jayne's fight of faith was always for more than just Fraser. It was for the hearts of their other three children—Josh and the girls, Amber who was three and Olivia who was just eighteen months. Adrian couldn't help but wonder what all of this was doing to them. He missed their home. They were raising their family in a hospital. Schooling happened here. Bill paying happened here. Meals. Family discussions. Deaths. All of that, everything, happened here.

Death was not supposed to invade a child's life.

This was not normal.

HE WAS BORN HEALTHY

When Fraser had been born, he was a healthy boy—9 pounds, 10 ounces. The first six weeks of his life were joyful chaos as Adrian and Jayne adapted to parenting four children. Adrian worked as a full-time firefighter and part-time pastor of a local church just outside of London. Jayne stayed home managing the children and the household, juggling all the schedules of a busy family.

Life was sleepless, of course, but good. *That was normal.*

But as Fraser approached six weeks, Jayne noticed a familiar pattern. She had seen this before. She had lived through all the fear once before. *No. Not again.*

"I took him to the doctor for a checkup. When they weighed him, I knew before they ever said it," Jayne remembered. "I hated the words *failure to thrive*. Olivia also had been healthy at birth, but at six weeks, quit thriving. One emergency room visit turned into six months of intense hospital trips and treatments. But she pulled through and lived to welcome her baby brother into this world. How could we go through this again? He had been so healthy for weeks. A perfectly normal baby."

Day after day, week after week, Fraser didn't put on even an ounce of weight. At six months old, he weighed exactly the same as at birth. His skin was blotchy. His stomach was swollen like a starving child. Every day felt like death was lingering, ready to swallow him, until one day it pounced.

"As we raced him to the hospital," Adrian recalled, "we had no idea if he *would* live or if he *could* live. As Jayne held Fraser's tiny body, even though she and I weren't holding each other physically, we were locked into this together. We didn't understand any of it, but we trusted God as we always had.

"We once heard a pastor say there was an eleventh commandment: 'Thou shalt bash on.' For Jayne and me, that became somewhat of an anchor for our souls. Through the years, when circumstances seemed more than our hearts could take, one of us would look at the other—usually Jayne to me—and say, 'Bash on.' We knew that meant to keep trusting in God and keep moving forward. It meant we would put our faith in God regardless of what we were going through. Regardless of what we didn't understand. We knew and believed that God was a good God and good is what he does—even when circumstances weren't good. We've always been determined to make every moment of our lives count—whether good or bad. Somehow, what we were going through had to have meaning."

When they arrived at the hospital, a team began to work on Fraser immediately. He quit breathing—twice. And what began as an emergency room visit turned into an eight-month stay. That day began a new life for their family that wouldn't feel normal again for years.

"I would go to work and then either go to the hospital to spend the night so Jayne could be home with our kids, or I would go home to look after our kids so she could spend the night at the hospital. We lived passing each other coming and going for eight months. And then when we didn't think it could get any worse, Fraser showed signs that we might lose him once and for all."

That's when they left their home and moved to Great Ormond Street Children's Hospital in London—a world-renowned facility specializing in pediatric healthcare and research. That's when they moved into a hospital apartment. That's when they first met all of the other children's families in the ward. That's when failure to thrive felt like it was going to infect them all.

WHAT'S NEXT?

Failure to thrive is a term that could be used to describe more than just infants who can't get enough nutrition or maintain a healthy weight. It equally could be used to describe our hearts when fear takes root and grows bigger than our faith, when fear so clouds our perspective that we can no longer see our faithful God—standing before us, ready and willing to guide us, ready to fight for us.

In every battle we face, fear is our fiercest enemy—and the enemy of our souls knows it. That's why he's always ready to foster it and reinforce it in our minds. If we don't learn how to overcome its power, then it can defeat us every time. It can even develop into chronic conditions that manifest in our bodies and minds, such as anxiety, panic attacks, incessant worry, or sleepless nights. If you have ever suffered from any of fear's debilitating effects, then you know that the symptoms are very real. What may start as a negative feeling or inner conflict can grow into an incapacitating challenge.

Fear can do all this.

Fear can diminish our willingness to risk. To dream. To try again. To believe again. Instead of declaring, we question. Instead of standing, we shrink. Instead of persevering, we quit. Instead of trusting, we worry. Instead of resting in God, we exhaust ourselves.

Fear can send us on a roller-coaster ride of emotions that leaves us reaching to control what always evades our grasp. That's how my father's journey with cancer was for our family. That's how it was for Adrian and Jayne during their year of fighting for Fraser.

If you've ever endured one crisis after another—if you've

ever felt hammered by the enemy—then you know what I'm talking about. If you've ever watched a loved one suffer a long-term illness or addiction, you've seen the "one step forward, two steps backward" rhythm that can happen. You know the challenge of believing for the best, while probably being told to prepare for the worst. You know what it's like to courageously cling to your faith, while gradually being conditioned by unexpected events to live in fear.

How many couples have finally managed to get pregnant, only to miscarry again? How many couples then have decided to adopt, been told a baby is available, and then the adoption falls through? How can someone facing repeated heartache not help but develop a gnawing, recurring thought, *What next?*

Fear does that.

It lies to us. It shrinks us. It builds dread into our hearts. It tempts us to believe there are no answers. *That the unexpected is something to fear.* That something is always lurking around the corner—like it was for Adrian and Jayne day after day.

But fear is not from God, and it's not more powerful than God. He knew it would come to steal our peace, not once or twice, but constantly throughout our lives. So, in his great mercy and faithfulness to us, God made a way for us to be more than equipped to overcome its effects and walk in faith. He gave us three offensive weapons to lean into when we're attacked: "For God has not given us a spirit of fear, but of *power* and of *love* and of *a sound mind*" (2 Timothy 1:7 NKJV, emphasis added).

This verse clearly shows us that fear is a spirit, but it's not from God. Every time fear tries to grip us, it's the enemy trying to take us down and terrify us out of trusting God. But the spirit of fear is no match for the Spirit of God who lives inside us.[1] God's Spirit is the source of our power. We can rely on, draw on, and walk in peace in the midst of fear and anxiety because the God who is in us is greater than anything or anyone that comes against us.[2] The Holy Spirit is who I turned to for strength when the doctor said, "Chris, you have cancer." He is there for you too, ready to help you, steady you, comfort you, and strengthen you in whatever unexpected challenge you face today.

When we rely on the Holy Spirit, we can take heart, because we are not fighting alone. We fight the good fight of faith in God's power, not by focusing on fear and trying to defeat it in our own strength, but by relying on God, knowing he is faithful. I came to realize that the more I trust my heavenly Father, the more fear is defeated in my heart and in my mind. If I focus on God more than the unexpected circumstance, then it is God who will be biggest in my heart and mind, and peace will be my outcome. When my doctor called, I could have easily spiraled into a dark pit when I began to think of what could happen to me and to our family, but I quickly focused my mind on God and what he could do. The path God has given us winds upward not downward, but we have to make him bigger to stay on that path mentally, emotionally, and physically.[3] That's what kept Adrian and Jayne from panicking every day.

God has also equipped us with love. Why love? Because he is love, and he is the greatest power of all. When we spend time in his presence, our fear acquires a terminal case of failure to thrive. In God there is no fear, because perfect love casts out all fear.[4] Personally, when I don't know what to do in a situation, I focus on how much he loves me. I remind myself that God is for me, with me, and will help me.

God wants us to believe his love, walk in his love, and be mentally at peace. That's the third weapon, which is having a sound mind. He doesn't want us to live tormented by fear's driving thoughts that lead to so much worry and stress. God has larger shoulders than we do, and he wants to carry our concerns for us. But we have to mentally hand them over to him. We have to cast our cares on him in prayer.[5] We cannot control the uncontrollable, but we can entrust all of it to God. God doesn't sleep or slumber, so sometimes I jokingly say, "If you see the devil, tell him I've gone to bed," but really, I'm not joking.[6] If God isn't sleeping, and he's watching over me, then there's no sense in both of us staying up. I know I can trust God to take care of all that I cannot control.

Adrian and Jayne practiced these principles to keep moving forward, but not all at once. They drew on what they needed for the moment, because trusting God is a process—a series of choices—not a one-time event. It's the ongoing journey called life. It's a cycle we repeat daily, hourly, sometimes even minute to minute, that leads to consistent growth. We overcome, get peace, but then get hit with another unexpected blow. But each time we go through the cycle, we grow stronger and more mature. That's why what used to rattle me doesn't even move me now. That's what was happening to Adrian and Jayne with every negative report, with every setback, with every threat of losing Fraser.

IT'S BOTH/AND

"We lived every moment of every day never knowing if Fraser would live because the doctors repeatedly told us he wouldn't last long," Jane recalls. "So, we took turns spending the night with him and staying with the other children in the apartment. I couldn't bear the thought of him dying and one of us not being there. And whichever one of us was with the other three would intentionally read to them before bed, anything to try to create some kind of normality. Every day we looked for something from God to get us through and give us good memories in such an awful place."

So, Adrian and Jayne kissed goodbye each night, fought the fear each day, and kept going.

They never knew what the next twenty-four hours would hold.

"The fear of Fraser dying was just as real as the fear of him living," Jayne said, "because we didn't know what that future would look like."

Profound. How many of us live our everyday lives fearful of the future just because we don't know what it will look like? When, truthfully, we cannot control the past, present, or future? Jesus spoke directly to our human tendency of fearing the unknown and worrying about the future when he said, "Can any one of you by worrying add a single hour to your life? . . . Therefore do not worry about tomorrow, for tomorrow will worry about itself. Each day has enough trouble of its own" (Matthew 6:27, 34).

God wants us to trust him in every minute of every day just as Adrian and Jayne did. They had to trust that every time Fraser took a breath, he'd take the next one. That level of trust is what God wants us to be anchored in all the time. When we expect instead of worry, then we can live with a heart full of hope. When we anticipate the best, instead of the worst, we can live faith-filled every day.

I believe God wants to teach us practical ways to trust him more in our everyday lives so that we won't live holding back. But, to be freed from this kind of fear, we will have to let him lead us one growth step at a time. That's what he did for

Adrian and Jayne, and he started teaching them long before Fraser was born.

"Adrian was a firefighter and the station where he worked was just a few blocks away," Jayne explained. "Early in our marriage, I would always hear the sirens blare when they got a call, and fear would grip me. I remember one day telling myself I just couldn't let fear rule over me like that. It was exhausting me. God spoke to me from Isaiah 43, and it became a promise for me to cling to about Adrian: 'When you walk through the fire, you will not be burned; the flames will not set you ablaze.' But I also thought, *If Adrian does die in a fire, then he died doing what God had called him to do.* I had to be both realistic *and* walk in faith."

I love that God taught Jayne it wasn't either/or. It was both/and. She knew the risks of Adrian's job that he loved, *and* she stood on God's promise for his safety. She understood we can step out in faith and still *feel* afraid. We can choose to believe God's Word, put our heart in his hands, and still have to resist the fear trying to take root inside. We can embrace the process and move forward, even if we take a few steps backward at the same time.

This strengthening of Jayne's faith is what ultimately enabled her to withstand the agonizing heartache of Fraser's illness. Some days she couldn't even touch her baby because he was so fragile; her touch could have sent him into cardiac arrest.

"I remember the moment when I didn't think I could endure any more of the suffering with Fraser," Jayne says. "Our lives had been out of control for such a long time and there was nothing we could do to fix it. I didn't know what else to pray. We had fasted, anointed him with oil—everything we'd ever learned. And most of those times, things only grew worse. I didn't know what else to think or say or do. And the Lord's Prayer rose up in my heart.[7] *Lord, give us our daily bread.*

It occurred to me that I could just focus on the daily bread. I could believe God for the next step and quit thinking about anything else. So, I began thanking God every day for daily bread. I thanked him for the small things. After almost a year of fighting for Fraser's life, that was all I could focus on."

God was showing Jayne how to trust him in every single moment—by receiving her daily bread. God doesn't promise us weekly, monthly, or annual bread. He promises us daily bread—bread for the moment. God was showing her how to overcome when she felt utterly overwhelmed, when fear was constantly trying to destabilize her heart. When she couldn't make sense of anything that was happening, when she felt like the circumstances were suffocating her and she couldn't come up for air. That's when God was saying: *Quit thinking about all you can't control and just focus on today. Just focus on what you can do, on what you can change, on what you can accomplish to move forward, even if you take steps back at the same time.* He was teaching her how to not be overwhelmed.

We've all been to that place where, just like Jayne, the enemy has knocked the wind out of us. God understands when we feel this way, and he inspired the Psalms to show us how to identify our feelings and move forward in faith so we can get up and breathe again. He wants us to know that it is okay to feel afraid, but it is dangerous to let ourselves be controlled by fear.

> Hear my cry, O God;
> Attend to my prayer.
> From the end of the earth I will cry to You.
> When my heart is overwhelmed;
> Lead me to the rock that is higher than I.
>
> PSALM 61:1–2 NKJV

The psalmist's heart had been broken, and it was so heavy, he poured out all his pain. That's what Jayne did when she felt that she couldn't endure anymore. Jayne knew that we live in a fallen world and because of that, there will always be problems we cannot solve, but we can take every single one of them to the One who can. She knew that she had to acknowledge how she really felt, and then take all those feelings and heartache to God.

When we feel like we're losing heart, God wants us to lean into him: "I have told you these things, so that *in me* you may have peace. In this world you will have trouble. But take heart! I have overcome the world" (John 16:33, emphasis added). In this verse, to "have trouble" means to be squashed. Unsolved problems, ongoing turmoil, tend to squash and suffocate us. They overwhelm us. They try to keep us in a state of perpetual fear, but we have to learn how to fight the good fight of faith in spite of how we feel.

"Today, when I look back, I can't imagine how much worse it would have been if we hadn't prayed," Jayne says, "if we hadn't anointed him with oil, and stood on God's promises. Faith is determined effort to absolutely believe that God can do anything, even when you don't see it. Even when it gets worse before it gets better. It's not denial. It's not hype. We knew Fraser could die, but we chose to believe God could heal him. And we knew if he did die, heaven would be his home. In reality, it was a win-win situation, because we would see him again someday, but of course, we wanted him healed here on earth.

"Oftentimes the doctors and nurses would ask us why we weren't hysterical. We had always prayed to be a family of influence. First Peter 2:12 says to live good lives so others will see your good works and glorify God. Whether Fraser lived or died, we were getting to influence others with the goodness of God. People knew we were real."

Jayne wasn't hysterical because she knew where to go when she felt overwhelmed. She resisted the spirit of fear and embraced the *sound mind* God had given her. She leaned into that sound mind so she wouldn't go out of her mind with worry and anxiety. She leaned into the *power* of the Holy Spirit to fight the good fight of faith, so she could take heart and have peace. She leaned into *love*—the greatest of all—and loved her children, her husband, the nurses and doctors. She loved and trusted God and his Word. She fell back on passages that had gotten her through tough times before.

"I remember how so many times I thought about the Bible story of the three young Hebrew men the king threw into the fire. They came out of it and didn't even smell like smoke.[8] Adrian always came home from the fire station and smelled like smoke." Jayne smiled. "But when Fraser got sick, I stood on these verses, and declared back to God in prayer that as we walked through this fire, we would not be burned, and we would not even smell of smoke."

GOD IS ALWAYS PREPARING US

At the threshold of every challenge—of every new opportunity for growth—the enemy will send a spirit of fear. I know that every time I've gone to another level—in ministry, in my personal spiritual growth, in relationships—I've faced fear. Every time I've determined to open another A21 office or expand the reach of Propel (our ministry helping women realize their purpose, passion, and potential), fear has been there to threaten me, push back at me, and oppose me. When my doctor said I had cancer, fear was right beside me. Taunting me. Tempting me. Trying to take me out. When Nick called one time to tell me he and the girls had been in a car accident, fear didn't disappoint. They didn't have life-threatening injuries, but fear was eager to race me down a road in seconds—if I had given in to it. I know firsthand the power of fear to intimidate, paralyze, and debilitate.

But we know God doesn't send fear. Instead, he equips us to resist fear by trusting him, just as I did during those ten weeks of waiting after I was diagnosed with cancer.

I've learned how every single one of my experiences, both the expected and the unexpected, is never wasted in God. I've learned how he uses them in my life—past and present—to prepare and to propel me into my future.

That's what he did with all that Adrian and Jayne experienced.

They learned that *confronting* fear never ends, but being *controlled* by fear can end. They learned to thrive internally, despite not seeing improvements externally. They allowed God to work in them, and that allowed God to work through them. He didn't cause Fraser's condition, but he didn't allow it to be wasted either. He was working through it to transform Adrian and Jayne, to train them to not become overwhelmed.

They faced fear daily for years. First with Olivia, then with Fraser. It could have destroyed them—their marriage, their family, their faith in God. But instead, they kept facing and fighting it, refusing to allow it take root in their hearts, and that attitude grew them into the incredible parents and leaders they are today.

Without even realizing it, they were living the fruit of the Spirit: love, joy, peace, patience, kindness, goodness, faithfulness, gentleness, and self-control.[9] No wonder the hospital staff were amazed they weren't hysterical. Imagine if in every fearful situation, we could be so anchored in God that the fruit of the Spirit were simply our most authentic response. Imagine if we displayed:

- Love in the midst of indifference
- Joy in the midst of sorrow
- Peace in the midst of chaos
- Patience in the midst of frenzy
- Kindness in the midst of cruelty
- Goodness in the midst of evil
- Faithfulness in the midst of carelessness
- Gentleness in the midst of hardness
- Self-control in the midst of a world spiraling out of control

Imagine how free we'd feel if we learned to truly believe that in every situation, trust was the antidote to fear, that consciously trusting God would cause our moments of anxiety and panic to be short-lived. Imagine if we could grow to a place where trusting him was our first reaction. "Trust in the LORD with all your heart and lean not on your own understanding; in all your ways submit to him, and he will make your paths straight" (Proverbs 3:5–6).

I believe if we did, then we would become overcomers who were never overwhelmed. We would become Christians who, when unexpected events occur, demonstrate the power, love, and sound mind God has given us. We would become believing believers who flourish instead of failing to thrive.

This is what God is calling us to. When unexpected challenges come, God wants the eyes of our faith to immediately look up, to scan the horizon for how he is going to use this for our gain, for our good, and for an intentional purpose to advance his kingdom. Imagine the power and strength we'd have if we all learned to face the unexpected and the fear it brings with unwavering trust in God. What if we learned to respond just as the Bible shows us? For everyone to see? Isn't that what Adrian and Jayne learned to do?

Jayne didn't let fear cripple her. Even when the fight for her faith was minute by minute, the fruit of the Spirit flowed out of her life. In an overwhelmingly unexpected crisis, she was light in a very dark place. Can you imagine what she and Adrian had to overcome to comfort the other families when their children didn't live? What courage. What compassion. What love.

They transformed the unexpected and unwanted place where they found themselves into a place of meaningful and powerful ministry, just like I did as I was sitting in waiting rooms full of cancer patients. Perhaps in the days in which we live, we can confound people by responding in faith instead of fear, by letting our lights shine so bright that they dispel all the darkness around us.

Adrian and Jayne were ordinary people who expected God to be with them all day, every day, in the midst of the unexpected. They let God be God in their lives. They let him prepare them for the short term and for the long term.

Because of their faithfulness, God orchestrated for them to join Nick and me and our A21 family almost a decade ago. God used every experience with Fraser to prepare Adrian to serve as our COO, to save lives failing to thrive through the tragedy of human trafficking. In that hospital, they were able to see through where they were, even in the darkest hours, and trust God for their future. They trusted that God somehow was going to use this situation for their good—and he did.

It's time for us to all live this way. I believe God wants us to get to a place of such great faith that we anticipate the gains that are coming into our lives as we continue to trust him no matter what we're facing. It's part of how we become more like Christ.

When Jesus was on the cross, facing death, he thought of more than his immediate suffering. He thought of more than the fierceness of the enemy's attack. He thought of us, and what his present circumstance would produce in our future. And he showed us how to live free from the fear that inevitably comes with the unexpected. Later, the apostle Peter drew on Christ's example when he wrote:

> Beloved, *do not think it strange* concerning the fiery trial which is to try you, as though some strange thing happened to you; but rejoice to the extent that you partake in Christ's sufferings, that when his glory is revealed, you may also be glad with exceeding joy.
> 1 PETER 4:12–13 NKJV, emphasis added

"Do not think it strange." We could read that as: *Do not be afraid of the unexpected. Do not think, What next?* Let's not allow fear to condition us to expect the worst. Instead, let's courageously move through every new event expecting God to do something great with our lives, trusting him at a new level of faith.

When we partake in Christ's sufferings, we resist the temptation of limiting God to our present understanding, believing that he is writing the story of our lives that will inevitably lead to a conclusion of victory. We resist the temptation to panic, to think it is the end, to lose hope for our future. We resist the pressure to worry and stress and be overcome. We resist giving in and quitting. Jesus's suffering on the cross was something he looked *through* to the rest of the story—our story—of redemption and salvation and triumph. Yes, he asked God to "let this cup pass from me," but he moved forward.[10] He mustered his strength, and though tempted with anxiety and fear, even to the point of sweating drops of blood, he still approached the cross fearlessly. He had an eternal perspective that is so different from our natural, short-term thinking.

When Adrian and Jayne's trial began just six weeks into Fraser's life, they had no way of knowing what was almost twenty years down the road. I'm sure at any point in their heartbreaking journey they would have loved for their cup of suffering to pass from them—first with Olivia and next with Fraser. But their absolute trust in a trustworthy God prepared them for what God had prepared for them—and all the lives they would help rescue.

A SUPERNATURAL ECLIPSE

Approaching a full year of fighting, Adrian and Jayne continued living between the hospital apartment and around Fraser's bed. And little changed.

"I was always honest with God, telling him that I didn't understand why all this was happening," Adrian confesses. "But at the same time, I believed in his promises to me and Jayne. We resisted fear every time it tried to grip our hearts. We were determined to bash on."

"I think you can learn from fear instead of letting it affect you," Jayne said. "It's like learning to escape a riptide current. We always taught our children that if they got caught in one at the beach to not panic and fight it, but swim parallel with it because it will eventually end and you can escape and swim back to shore. Yes, we resist fear, but the way we fight it is to learn from it by first facing it so it loses its paralyzing effect. We recognize it for what it is and somehow let God grow us in the midst of it. And when we do, he'll help us get back to shore."

One day, a leader from Adrian and Jayne's church came by. He wanted to pray for Fraser. Not a day had gone by that someone hadn't prayed. As the man prayed, a solar eclipse over London blanketed the sky in darkness. As the eclipse passed and light shone again, something shifted.

When Fraser was weighed the next day, he had gained one-half of one ounce. It was as though he'd experienced a supernatural eclipse—a passing from darkness to light. To Adrian and Jayne, it was a miracle. He moved from being overshadowed by darkness to gradually coming alive. They were amazed that he continued to gain weight every day after that. He began to thrive!

"After four and a half months at Great Ormond Street Children's Hospital," Adrian said, "they decided Fraser was thriving enough to send us home. It had been a full year since we'd first raced him to the emergency room. He was the only one from the ward who ever went home. We still came back for weekly visits, and we learned to inject nutrition into his body through a tube in his side every four hours—*for the next four years*. We jokingly called it his 'rocket fuel,' and it smelled awful, but we didn't care. He was thriving."

Fraser was ten years old before he was completely off all medication. He was twelve when he finally got to attend a local school. Today, he is a lean six-foot-one tall student in his third year of apprenticeship in landscape construction. He plays rugby, drives his own car, and serves as a youth leader at church. He has two small scars on his abdomen that testify to his fragile first years of life.

For Adrian and Jayne, they truly learned to leave fear behind and move forward in faith—and they've embraced every assignment God has prepared for them with great faith.

Today, when Adrian looks into the hollow eyes of a rescued young girl in A21's care, he doesn't see her emaciated soul, her atrophied mind, or her barely pumping heart. He doesn't declare that she has a hopeless diagnosis—*a failure to thrive*.

He knows better. No matter how many days, weeks, months, or years, he knows she'll come back to life. One day, there'll be a supernatural eclipse—a turning point. Darkness will turn to light. All because of trusting God—no matter what—and never giving up. All because of believing that unexpected events in our lives can be used for great gain. For new levels of faith. For new adventures in God.

Chapter Three

WHEN THE UNEXPECTED DISAPPOINTS

Rising Up in Resilience

─────

Most people want to be circled by safety, not by the
unexpected. The unexpected can take you out. But the
unexpected can also take you over and change your life.
Put a heart in your body where a stone used to be.
—RON HALL

Sinking further into the couch as the room dimmed gray from the setting sun, Amanda stared blankly at her phone as though at any moment a text would reveal all the answers— and save her. Not from hell or damnation. From herself. There was no more energy to cry. No strength to pick up her heart. No muscle to move off the couch.

Like flirting with a bad high school boy, she teased her pain with temptations of how she could end it all and never feel anything ever again. Not the thrilling highs. Not the crashing lows that always followed. She never wanted to repeat this cycle. Not one more time. Not one more experience of . . .
Something wonderful ending abruptly.

Something hopeful failing unexpectedly.

Something promising collapsing quickly.

All roads leading back to, *What's wrong with me?*

Mr. Right turning out to be all wrong.

Sitting in the shadows all alone. Again.

Numbness gradually shrouded her mind like someone pulling a sheet over her body until it finally covered her head. It would be so easy to . . . *just let go.*

Slowly pulling a throw pillow to her chest like a life preserver, Amanda held on for her life.

How did I get here?

This isn't who I am.

God, help me.

As the cloud of disappointment threatened to overtake her, Amanda felt suddenly shocked back to life by a primal instinct to survive. She reached out. Her hands shaking and her heart racing, she texted a friend who was going through an equally hard time, "Hey, how are you?"

"No, how are *you?*" her friend instantly replied.

How am I? she thought. Amanda honestly didn't know the answer. This was all so unexpected. This was not how she had ever imagined her life would unfold.

ODD GIRL OUT

Amanda had always been a strong person, certainly not someone given to such hopelessness. But, like all of us, she felt like she could only take so much pain and disappointment before she hit a place of complete despair.

Most of us don't grow up knowing how to process deep

feelings of rejection in a healthy way, so we move through heartbreaking moments, piling up our pain and storing it in our hearts—until our hearts can't contain one more ounce of heartache. That's when we sometimes turn to coping in destructive ways. We simply want the pain to stop, and the feelings of hopelessness and despair to end.

That's what happened to Amanda. She grew up in in a tiny Southern US town of eight hundred people—the kind where everyone knows everyone and all their business. The kind where everyone attended church from the time they were babies. The kind where everyone grew up to marry a high school or college sweetheart. Everyone except Amanda.

That was when Amanda first remembers the hurt of disappointment trying to take up residence in her heart.

"Growing up, I remember always thinking, *I can't wait to be a wife!* I felt like God put that desire deep within me—and yet, I always had an awareness that it wouldn't happen in the normal way for me—whatever normal is. But I always trusted God. I knew I wanted to be married, and in our community, getting married was just as expected as breathing or going to school or work or church. It wasn't said aloud, but you weren't perceived as complete or to have even started your adult life until you were married.

"When my brother graduated from high school in May, he married in July. When my oldest sister graduated from high school in May, she married in June. When my next sister finished college—she married right after graduation. I went to college and graduated and was still single. I became the odd girl out."

As the years went by, Amanda kept trusting God, but being single grew into the heaviest burden she had ever known.

And the repeated disappointments from failed relationships became as familiar as Sunday dinners.

"It was a mystery no one ever let you forget," Amanda said as she described year after year of being single. "Every family get-together included *the quiz*: 'Amanda, when are you going to get married? Have you met anyone lately? Maybe you are expecting too much in a man. Have you seen John's cousin Joe lately? He is really cute.'

"There was no dodging *the quiz*.

"My friends and family meant well. They loved me, but they treated my singleness like a condition to cure. My heart wanted to be open to any and all good advice, but their suggestions chipped away at my confidence. When they suggested I was too intimidating, I would think, *What does that mean anyway? Why should I have to minimize who God created me to be so a man doesn't feel insecure around me? I don't want a guy I have to prop up by putting myself down.* They would suggest that I needed to try harder. *How do I 'try harder'?* They would say that I was too picky. That was always the hardest thing to hear. As much as I tried to be grateful for their concern, my heart felt like it was working overtime to stay positive. I did trust God, but walking it out every day in real life wasn't easy."

Amanda didn't date too many guys through the years, but she dated enough to know the chronic heartache of when people—and life—fail us.

Her first serious boyfriend was also the first to break her heart. We'll call him Mr. Go-to-Jail: "He was the first guy I opened my heart to. He came from a great family, fit in nicely with ours, but totally led a double life." Amanda winced. "So, he went to jail, and I went to college. I never could quite let my heart be fully open again until years later."

Then there was Mr. Gonna-Make-Money: "He was everything your mama wants you to bring home to meet the family," Amanda remembered. "He'd finished medical school and was starting his residency. He was financially stable. Charming. Successful. People in the church thought we were a darling couple—and the expectations grew. But over the months, I realized that he didn't want to pursue the Lord in the same way I did. It was so painful to leave the security of a man and to choose Jesus, but I knew I had to."

There was Mr. Let's-Just-Be-Friends: "I couldn't lie to myself," Amanda admitted. "I wanted our relationship to work so badly. I was so tired of the pressure of wanting to be married, of wanting to end all the feelings of the unknown, of always looking and wondering, of wanting to be seen and known and loved. I wanted to belong to someone. I wanted someone to hold me at the end of every day. But I knew he wasn't the one, so we parted ways as friends."

Eventually, there was the real Prince Charming, Mr. Too-Good-to-Be-True: Love. Romance. Thoughtfulness. Pursuit. Security. He seemed to provide it all. But it turned out to be a storybook romance without the storybook ending. The night they broke up was the final blow to her heart—the one that knocked all the life out of her.

That day was the culmination of almost a decade of dating that seemingly led nowhere. It was hard for Amanda to feel so successful in fulfilling her purpose, so fortunate in her friendships, but suffer one unexpected loss after another in dating. She had graduated from college, was consistently promoted in her work, was loved by everyone at her church, adored by her family. Definitely a viable catch. But when she couldn't make sense of why so many relationships unexpectedly failed, she plummeted emotionally. Even though she'd grown up in a great Christian home and served God in ministry for years, she had no idea how to manage the repeated disappointment. She had no idea how to refuse to allow the disappointment to cause her to retreat internally, shrink in her faith, and become fearful, unable to fully trust.

So, ten months after meeting Mr. Too-Good-to-Be-True, there she sat on the couch unable to respond to her friend's text message. The disappointment—and all the disappointments before that—had a crippling effect and the thoughts swirled, *What's wrong with me? Why am I always the odd girl out?*

STILL SINGLE

Like Amanda, I know exactly what it feels like to be in my late twenties and single, to be the odd girl out in a group where every friend was married and most had children. I remember being so lonely at times, desperately wanting to fulfill my purpose and not compromise the call of God on my life in any way, and wondering if it was possible to be married as well.

From the time I was small, I was the anomaly in my big, loud Greek family—and I'm talking so big that even third cousins were at every family gathering. While Amanda's polite Southern family broke bread at Sunday dinners, mine was breaking plates! We were volatile. Celebratory. Chaotically fun. And typical of Greek culture, *all* my big family felt it was their responsibility and right to all be involved in the success—or failure—of my personal life. We really were like that. Big. Loud. Greek. Just like the movie. Yes, that one.

Getting married and having babies was paramount for a

good Greek girl. That was success in my parents' eyes, and to ensure my winning future, they even betrothed me to a young man like a bartered business deal. It was that critical to them that I secure a husband—and as early as possible.

But being an independent girl who liked to read, play soccer with the boys, and be the leader, made me . . . well, not exactly a desirable traditional Greek wife.

"Christina," my mother would lament, "how many times do I have to tell you that boys don't like smart girls or rough girls? For you to get married, the boys need to see you in the kitchen cooking—not reading a book."

But this passion of my parents to get me married hit a wall when I was accepted to Sydney University at eighteen—one of my greatest dreams at the time. Horrified I would be more educated than my future husband, my fiancé's parents sat me down and told me if I pursued my education and earned a degree, then I could not marry their son. Truthfully, I wanted to be married, but at that time, I wanted to go to college more. So I did the unthinkable. I chose the unexpected. I chose college and stayed single—for many, many more years.

To say my mother and every single one of my aunts were not pleased when I ended the relationship with my betrothed is an understatement. I was an utter failure in their eyes, but I knew in my gut it was right, even though it was so countercultural to everything I was raised to be.

Although I met Nick a decade later and eventually married him, in that moment, I felt like a failure on so many levels, and simultaneously like a success on so many others. I was college bound, determined, ambitious, courageous. Yet, I was single. And *old* by my family's standards. The question always on their minds was, *What's wrong with her?*

Sounds familiar. Amanda was a success—bright, pretty, educated, loved Jesus with all her heart—and yet singleness made her *feel* that she was less than a success. As though something was wrong with her. But she kept trusting God—and she bravely kept dating.

STUCK IN A MOMENT

As the years go by, and we wait for our dreams to come to pass, it takes courage: to keep trusting God, to keep our hearts open and tender, and to keep risking and trying again. At the beginning of any journey, it's easier to be full of zeal and keep a positive attitude. That's how Amanda started out with her desire to be a wife. She was full of expectant hope.

But then something happened. The first real boyfriend hurt her. And she withdrew, unable to completely open up again for the next few years.

Something similar happened to you—and me. Someone disappointed us. Something unexpected happened. Or, as in Amanda's life, the expected she had hoped for, longed for, lived for *didn't* happen. Either way, people—and life—failed us.

That kind of disappointment is inevitably going to happen to all of us, because the enemy is going to make sure we get hit by at least a few unexpected blows that knock us off our feet. He's going to do whatever he can to stop our hopes for the best and to start our expectations for the worst. He's going to reinforce the belief that if we step out and risk our heart again, people will fail us again. And little by little, we move out of faith and into fear—and disappointment settles in our heart and shrinks our dreams. And over time, that disappointment leads us to doubt and pull back. We withdraw to protect ourselves from ever risking hurt again.

We grow numb.

We stop trusting in God's promise to us—or doubt that we ever heard it in the first place.

Disappointment—that let-down feeling where our emotions bottom out and our faith does too—is a powerful destructive force. It can leave us stuck in a painful moment through which we filter and even forfeit future experiences. It is a force we have to face and overcome to live a life full of faith embracing the unexpected.

It's a lesson I learned from an experience with my girls. When they were younger, and because we live in Southern California and get a huge resident discount, frequent trips to Disneyland were the perfect mini-vacations. I remember one visit that altered my pixie dust dreams for a long time.

Now, the story I'm about to tell you is definitely lighthearted, but the truth of what I learned about the crippling power of disappointment—and how we have to get unstuck—was very deep, and I've applied this lesson to my life ever since.

Hopping on one ride after another in Fantasyland, Sophia and I boarded our pirate ship at Peter Pan's Flight teeming with excitement—mostly because I didn't do scary adult rides and she was still young enough to think Peter Pan was awesome. As the ride took off, we immediately flew through the Darling children's bedroom and out into the dark London sky. The music filled the darkness: "You can fly. You can fly. You can fly." The stars twinkled as we flew past Big Ben. Windows in the buildings below glowed as the wind rushed by our faces. Then suddenly, there it was.

Neverland.

As we readied ourselves to see the interior of the island, watch the Lost Boys battle Captain Hook, delight in fairies and the infamous crocodile, surprisingly, our fantasy came to an abrupt halt.

The music waned to a garbled muffle.

The darkness was disrupted by a flashing amber glow.

Our pirate ship jerked to a stop.

As our senses adjusted to the changes, and our eyes to the emergency lighting, our ship began to rock ever so slowly forward. Then, as we took in our surroundings, we could see everything—*everything we're not supposed to see*. What had appeared so real only moments before, suddenly wasn't.

The stars were gone.

The moon didn't glow.

Neverland was an illusion.

I was actually disappointed.

But not Sophia. She was pointing out all the characters. She didn't care that the ride wasn't all that was promised. Perceiving my shock, she sought to comfort me: "It's okay, Mummy; these things happen. Can we go on the Alice in Wonderland ride now?"

As I numbly got off the ride and we made our way to the next one, my expectations of hopeful adventure began to wane.

Over the coming months, I found I didn't enjoy visits to the park in quite the same way. I spent more time on my phone, lost in my own world, while Sophia and Catherine rode the rides together. Because of one negative experience, I spent less time engaging in the moment—which meant missing out on life with my girls.

As silly as it sounds, I was disillusioned. I had been disappointed.

Yes, it was shallow, and maybe you're rolling your eyes at me right now, but the struggle was real.

And the life lesson so powerful.

Sophia managed her disappointment well.

I did not.

She was resilient.

I was *stuck in a moment*.

We had the exact same experience but two totally different responses.

We had the exact same experience but ended up in two different places emotionally.

No wonder Jesus said, "Truly I tell you, anyone who will not receive the kingdom of God like a little child will never enter it" (Mark 10:15). If we are going to fulfill our purpose and keep on loving the adventure, then we must accept that some things will break down along the way.

The ride may jerk to a surprising stop.

Dim emergency lighting may be all we have to light our way through a dark season.

Or, the harsh lights of reality may *all* come on—much like the moments when Amanda realized in each relationship that "he wasn't the one"—and we realize that life is not what we thought it would be . . .

- The career path we'd followed dead-ends.
- The event we'd planned for months flops.
- The opportunity we'd risked everything to pursue evaporates.

When life doesn't go our way—which it rarely does—and when our expectations lead to utter disappointment, we don't always know how to recover our wonder of trusting God. When disappointments happen repeatedly, our hearts can grow sick and our thoughts can grow dark. That's when the enemy can move in and steal the last of our hope. That's when doubt and unbelief can overtake what's left of our faith—as happened to Amanda.

RECOVER YOUR WONDER

God had placed the desire to be married inside Amanda at a young age, and she had the expectation she would be. So, year after year, she had trusted God. Yet, year after year, she remained single. Eventually, it became hard to reconcile her desires with God's timing. Ultimately, that was the disappointment she couldn't get through alone.

God wants us to believe and understand that his promises don't have expiration dates. They aren't like passports or gym memberships. They aren't like the condiments in the fridge or the food in the pantry. Our heavenly Father has given us a book full of his promises that have no expiration dates—and he will always make good on his promises.

Holding to our faith—even in the face of deep disappointment—is critical. Making God's promises bigger than our disappointments is essential. Getting into his Word and letting it get into us brings our hearts back to life. Worshiping him opens the door for the Holy Spirit to encourage us and heal us so we can trust again. Learning how to change our perspective through steps like these helps us transition from fearing the unexpected to trusting God through it.

Do we trust that God is who he says he is?

Do we trust that God will do what he says he will do?

Do we trust that God is working all things together for our good and his glory?

Do we trust that he who promised is faithful?

Until we change our perspective, we won't see things clearly, and we'll even miss God ministering directly to us— much like the two disciples who walked together in sorrow along the Emmaus road.

The two disciples, who were leaving Jerusalem heartbroken and bitterly disappointed, had followed Jesus and trusted him, only to be shocked and disillusioned by his crucifixion. All their hope had been in Jesus, and how he was the one to redeem Israel. But their dreams had died on the cross with Jesus.

Now that same day two of them were going to a village called Emmaus, about seven miles from Jerusalem. They were talking with each other about everything that had happened. As they talked and discussed these things with each other, *Jesus himself came up and walked along with them; but they were kept from recognizing him.*

He asked them, "What are you discussing together as you walk along?"

They stood still, *their faces downcast.* One of them, named Cleopas, asked him, *"Are you the only one visiting Jerusalem who does not know the things that have happened there in these days?"*

"What things?" he asked.

"About Jesus of Nazareth," they replied. "He was a prophet, powerful in word and deed before God and all the people. The chief priests and our rulers handed him over to be sentenced to death, and they crucified him;

but we had hoped that he was the one who was going to redeem Israel. And what is more, it is the third day since all this took place. In addition, some of our women amazed us. They went to the tomb early this morning but didn't find his body. They came and told us that they had seen a vision of angels, who said he was alive. Then some of our companions went to the tomb and found it just as the women had said, but they did not see Jesus."

He said to them, "How foolish you are, and how slow to believe all that the prophets have spoken! *Did not the Messiah have to suffer these things and then enter his glory?" And beginning with Moses and all the Prophets, he explained to them what was said in all the Scriptures concerning himself.*

As they approached the village to which they were going, Jesus continued on as if he were going farther. But they urged him strongly, "Stay with us, for it is nearly evening; the day is almost over." So he went in to stay with them.

When he was at the table with them, he took bread, gave thanks, broke it and began to give it to them. *Then their eyes were opened and they recognized him, and he disappeared from their sight.* They asked each other, "Were not our hearts burning within us while he talked with us on the road and opened the Scriptures to us?"

They got up and returned at once to Jerusalem. There they found the Eleven and those with them, assembled together and saying, "It is true! The Lord has risen and has appeared to Simon." Then the two told what had happened on the way, and how Jesus was recognized by them when he broke the bread.

LUKE 24:13–35, emphasis added

These disciples had been with Jesus the week before his crucifixion and were full of hope. But when he was crucified, they lost all hope and headed back home to Emmaus. Their world came apart because the events did not unfold as they had anticipated. Even with all the rumors of the resurrection, they still did not believe Jesus was alive.

Their journey through disappointment and disillusionment to renewed hope is often the same path we follow:

- *Jesus began talking to them, but they could not recognize his voice.*[1] How many times does he speak to our hearts, yet we're so lost in our own concerns that we cannot hear him?
- *Their eyes were downcast.*[2] They were crushed and couldn't even look up to see the fellow traveler walking alongside them. As long as we look down at our circumstances, and not up at him, we'll miss what it is that we need to see—what he wants us to see.
- *They asked the only one who really knew what had happened if he had any idea of the disappointing events.*[3] When we finally ask God what he thinks, we open the door for the clarity only he can bring.
- *He brought them back to the Word.*[4] Jesus knew the promises of God and explained how those promises would be fulfilled in a way that would change the world. He told them that a new kingdom was at hand. It is always the Word that changes our perspective from disappointment to hope.
- *Finally, they saw him in the midst of their disappointment.*[5] How powerful it is when we can look up and see God, even when our circumstances are ongoing.
- *They got up at once. Their wonder came back.*[6] When our hope is renewed, we are strengthened to move forward.

Jesus always walks with us through our disappointment. Through our heartaches. Leading us to recover our wonder. Leading us to something better ahead. He is the one who helps us remember that although the unexpected happened to us, he'll never leave us.

Jesus was there for me in every unexpected disappointment.

He was there for Adrian and Jayne.

He was there for Amanda.

And he is there for you. Right now. Wherever you are.

MANAGING DISAPPOINTMENT

We all experience disappointments. All of us have expectations, whether big or small, that have not been met:

- Friends break their word.
- Our marriage ends.
- A colleague betrays us.
- Our kids don't turn out like we hoped.
- We never have the child we long for.
- We never find our soul mate.
- We don't get the promotion.
- We lose our retirement fund.
- A dream turns into a nightmare.
- We disappoint ourselves by saying or doing something we regret.

But despite how we feel, all the disappointment in the world will never change the promises of God, the reality of Jesus, or his destiny for our lives. None of our broken dreams, personal heartaches, or shattered plans can stop his desire for us to fulfill our purpose. The disappointment is real. The consequences can be devastating. To keep moving forward, we must learn to be resilient, like Sophia. We must learn to trust, like a little child. We must learn to manage our disappointments well, so we can hop on another ride full of renewed hope. Otherwise, while we're stuck in the disappointment behind us, we'll miss the adventure God is setting before us.

I don't know why Amanda is still single—and neither does she—but we both trust him.

I don't know why I had a miscarriage between having my two girls, but I trust him.

I don't know why women and men are trafficked all over the world, but I trust him—and I choose to be part of the solution.

I don't know why I wasn't miraculously and instantly healed of cancer, but I am thankful for all I went *through* to be well.

I don't know what has broken down along the way in your life. I don't know why your life has experienced unexpected events, but will you join me in trusting God once again?

What one experience has stopped you in your tracks?

What one experience has shaken you to your core and stolen all your confidence?

What one experience have you believed disqualifies you for the purpose to which God called you?

Do you see how it's what we *do* with our disappointments that determines our destiny? If we don't go *through* our hardships, we may move on in years, but our life stops at the point of our greatest disappointment. We either go *through* what happens and manage the disappointments well, or they manage us.

Sophia managed her disappointment—and mine—well. But I didn't. Because of one experience—just one experience—

my future adventures at Disneyland were tainted. I showed up physically but not mentally. I began missing out on precious time with my girls because I wasn't engaged in the moment. I let disappointment manage me, my emotions, and my responses.

I remember the day God told me to put my phone away and be present. The girls had hopped on a ride together, and as I watched them take off laughing and squealing, I realized how I wanted to be living that moment on the ride with them—totally carefree. I didn't want to be checking my phone and catching up on emails. As I stood there, wondering how I'd gotten off course, God took me back to that moment on Peter Pan's Flight and showed me how, though I hadn't really realized it, I'd let one experience alter my viewpoint. I had become stuck in a moment and my perspective of disappointment had caused me to disengage from an important purpose—to be present with and enjoy Catherine and Sophia.

Has it ever occurred to you that, if you'll revisit your disappointment, God can give you a new perspective on it—one that can become a tool to help others? That you can take what he gives to you and pass it on? This is the very principle the apostle Paul describes in his second letter to the church at Corinth:

> Praise be to the God and Father of our Lord Jesus Christ,
> the Father of compassion and the God of all comfort,
> who comforts us in all our troubles, so that we can comfort those in any trouble with the comfort we ourselves receive from God.
>
> 2 CORINTHIANS 1:3–4

Has it ever occurred to you that God can use your disappointments to set a new trajectory for you, one that gets you closer to your destiny? That's something I've experienced over and over again. All the disappointments in my life have ultimately become tools I could use to serve others. I will not let the enemy get the last word, because I believe there are divine appointments beyond all our disappointments. This was a lesson Amanda learned as well.

A DATE WITH DESTINY

When Amanda broke up with Mr. Too-Good-to-Be-True, she never saw him again.

"I remember telling God, 'I didn't need that,'" Amanda said.

"And I felt like God replied, 'You *exactly* needed that.'

"For two months, I was embarrassed, in shock, hurt, angry, grieving. And then the disappointment in my personal life spilled over into my work and leadership. I realized deep down that I was disappointed professionally, and even spiritually. I thought, *If this is living, I really don't want to live anymore.* But deep down I knew that wasn't God's will for my life. It wasn't truth. God was using the disappointment of another breakup to reveal other issues rooted in my heart. And I knew I needed to process all of this in a healthy and therapeutic way. It was this perfect storm of feeling like a failure in every area of life that finally pushed me to seek out a Christian counselor. I knew I needed someone who could help me sort through all the painful emotions, thoughts, and questions that were bombarding me."

I love how Amanda refused to stay stuck in that place of despair by taking the steps she needed to find healing and wholeness. Amanda is now thirty-six and still dating. Her pursuit of God is still unrelenting.

"I met a guy at the beach recently," Amanda said. "A perfect gentleman. After we'd dated a month or so, I told the Lord, 'God, I don't want to walk down this road unless I know it will have a good outcome. I don't want to go through pain again.'

"And God was so clear: *You'll never know without walking the road. There will always be hurt. You'll be hurt if it works out, and you'll be hurt if it doesn't. Relationships aren't about the end result. They're about what I have in them for you. For both of you. I give you to each other for each other, even if only for a season. Isn't that enough? Do you trust me with the process?*"

Do you see the shift in perspective? From selfish to unselfish. From resisting fear to embracing faith. From anxiety about the unexpected to trusting God even more. All the result of a perfect storm that led to a perfect transformation—which is the process of growth the apostle Paul describes as "working out our salvation." He writes:

> Therefore, my dear friends, as you have always obeyed—not only in my presence, but now much more in my absence—continue to work out your salvation with fear and trembling, for it is God who works in you to will and to act in order to fulfill his good purpose.
>
> PHILIPPIANS 2:12–13

Trusting God is a series of choices, not a one-time event. And it requires something of us, which is why Paul calls it "work." It's means choosing, again and again and again, to:

- Stay connected to God and his process. Daily.
- Process disorientation through God's perspective. Immediately.

- Risk, be vulnerable, and believe. Resiliently.
- Ask God for help when we don't have the answers. Courageously.

Choosing to trust God is part of how we live an intentional life. We choose not to avoid disappointment. Not to avoid pain. But rather to learn to manage our disappointments well, and to embrace the truth that the new adventure ahead looks different than we expected.

Disappointment is a place we pass through, not a place we stay. God wants us emotionally engaged in his purposes. Living in the moment. Fully alive. Hopeful. He wants us to let him restore our hearts, so we can keep moving forward and fulfill his good purpose for our lives. Even when people—and life—fail us.

Chapter Four

WHEN THE UNEXPECTED BETRAYS

Forgiving Freely

Loss is the uninvited door that extends us an
unexpected invitation to unimaginable possibilities.
—CRAIG D. JONESBOROUGH

M ummy," Sophia quietly began as she smoothed out the
covers on her bed and fidgeted with the edge. "Angela
invited the girls to her house a couple weekends ago . . . but
not me."

Staring at the ceiling as I lay beside her, I hid my initial
reaction behind my "listening face." Inside, my heart winced
with pain at the sting of her being excluded by the rest of "the
girls"—a group of friends who did everything together. And I
could feel what was coming next.

"She's been talking about me," Sophia said as her lips
began to tremble. "She made fun of me the other day in front
of everyone, and then they all walked off together without me."

We'd just lain down on Sophia's bed to talk and pray before
she went to sleep; it was one of my favorite times of day with

my baby girl. She'd been unusually quiet around the house for almost a week—completely out of character for a child who talks or sings every waking hour of the day. She had been withdrawn, lost her spark, and seemed anxious—definitely not herself. Sophia is highly sensitive and deep, but normally, she is quirky, happy, and fun-loving. She loves theater and acts out everything from Broadway plays to historical speeches. Boldly. Loudly. Joyfully. For the whole world to hear.

Because she'd been unusually quiet, I'd gently probed a few times, trying to get her to open up, but she'd deflected each time, denying anything was wrong. Typical of a kid at that age. Nonetheless, my mothering antennae remained up and on high alert, watching and praying over whatever it was. I had been patiently waiting for something to come to light, for the moment she would be ready to talk. I knew it would only be a matter of time.

Now it was spilling out all over the place.

"I saw them all pointing at me when we were at play practice after school." Sophia sobbed and choked out more of the story. "I know they were talking about me, because they don't think I'm as good as some of the other girls."

Her tender heart was utterly broken, and the more she talked, the more mine was too. I could hear her confusion as she tried so hard to sort out all her feelings and make sense of how they had acted. I could feel how helpless she was to find resolve. How she no longer felt like she belonged. I wanted so badly just to hold her and absorb all her pain so she wouldn't have to go through any of this.

"They act like they don't want me around," Sophia cried. "I don't even know why."

Inside, I cried too. I knew she had no way of knowing what

they had actually said, but she didn't have to. She knew the spirit of it—and as much as I hesitated to admit it—I did too. My stomach wrenched at the thought of her watching them and realizing she was at the center of their conversation. I could just see her sweet freckled face reddened with shame, completely at a loss about what to do because she'd been unexpectedly singled out and left out. I could see her standing there dazed from being so blindsided, unable to defend herself. If only I could have been there to catch all the flaming daggers before they pierced her heart. I imagine she fought bravely to swallow burning tears that day—just like I was trying to do now.

It would have been much easier on my heart for those girls to have taken a swing at me than at my baby girl. She had been so good to them—all of them. The care I'd seen her take picking out their birthday presents. The way she lit up when they were all together. *How could they?*

As I held onto Sophia, wanting to comfort and soothe her, I really was consoling both of us. I just wanted to make all the hurt go away. I had been through this with Catherine just a few years earlier, and I was well aware that some things about middle school never change.

I wanted to be angry with Angela—with all of them—but I knew what Sophia didn't. Angela's mom and dad were going through a painful divorce—trying to navigate a new normal in a place they'd never expected to be, trying to mend their own broken hearts at the same time they were caring for Angela's. I had no idea how this was all affecting Angela, but I felt sure she was most likely acting out of her own pain of adjusting to all the change. Her world had been shaken, and she was helpless to stop it.

As I considered what to say and where to begin, I decided

to keep it light for the moment. There would be plenty more conversations in the future, for middle school drama never seems to end. Tonight, Sophia needed love, comfort, and sleep. So, I made her laugh, reminded her of who she was in Christ, and reassured her of how much her family loved her and how all the other girls at school liked her so much. I explained how sometimes our friends have a bad day, or a bad week, and sometimes even a bad year. And before I left her room, I put on her absolute favorite soundtrack and let her sing all of it to me. By the time she fell asleep, she was happy. And I was relieved.

I KNEW HER PAIN

God made us for relationships—and he made relationships for us. He created us to be connected to him and to live our lives in community with others. Despite the fractures that can occur from differences of opinion or perspective, friendship is truly one of God's greatest gifts to us. That's what I wanted Sophia to learn most of all.

I love people with a passion and am deeply committed to my friends. I can't imagine doing life without my girlfriends. They are such a source of joy, companionship, and inspiration for me. I am loyal to my old friends, and I love making new ones—and most of all, I love introducing my friends to my other friends so that they will become friends.

The only challenge is that having friends and being a friend requires interacting with real-life human beings—human beings with quirks, flaws, emotions, challenges, baggage, and expectations. It's understandable why our relationships can get messy sometimes.

I wish I could have told Sophia that after middle school all her relational challenges would end and that she would live happily ever after. But I knew it wasn't true. This journey of following Jesus means that if we are going to keep our hearts open, soft, sensitive, and connected to humanity, then we must realize that we are never going to be bullet-proof to unexpected pain and heartache. No matter how carefully we pick our friends. No matter how long we've known them. No matter how old we are.

I once had a dear friend whom I loved wholeheartedly and with whom I shared so many fun times. We had endless heart-to-heart talks about God, ministry, life, family, fashion, movies, books, food, and of course, coffee. We shared an incredibly strong bond. We could talk about the most serious issues on earth one moment and then be laughing hysterically the next. She was one of those people with whom I didn't have to second-guess my words or filter my responses. There was simply an ease between us. And we had just enough differences to keep our friendship interesting, engaging, and evolving. She was one of the people I could call for anything, a true BFF.

Until the day she just wasn't.

She cut me off. No warning. No conversation. No explanation.

I felt just like Sophia. Bewildered. Confused. Shocked. I tried to make sense of it all, but no matter how many memories and conversations I relived, it still didn't make sense. I had let her into my inner world, into my heart. I had let her into the space where she had the power to wreck my heart, and she did. I had trusted her, bared my soul, risked being seen by her, and she had rejected me. Perhaps there is no greater pain between friends than the pain of being seen and then unexpectedly rejected.

When she cut me off, I felt so lost about what to do, what to say, and how to respond—just like a middle school girl. I felt as though I had been knocked off my feet, dumped on the floor, and left gasping for air, and I needed God to help me catch my next breath. I needed him to help me process the hurt and wrap my mind around what seemed incomprehensible. *How could she do this?* She was my friend. I loved her and had shared so much of my life with her. We both loved Jesus and wanted to see his kingdom flourish. How was this possible?

Rejection was the last thing I expected from someone I had trusted the most. I felt like King David when he penned gut-wrenching words about his own dear friend:

> If an enemy were insulting me,
> I could endure it;
> if a foe were rising against me,
> I could hide.
> But it is you, a man like myself,
> my companion, my close friend,
> with whom I once enjoyed sweet fellowship
> at the house of God,
> as we walked about
> among the worshipers.
>
> PSALM 55:12–14

Like David, I felt gutted to be on the receiving end of a severed relationship when I wasn't even sure why it ended. And all of it triggered the rejection of my past. That was the Achilles' heel of my soul—all the rejection and abandonment I had experienced as a child, all the shame. My knee-jerk response was to shut down and pull back. To draw a line in the sand and never let anyone cross it again. To erect a wall around my heart and never again let anyone in.

But I knew better and I wanted to do better. I knew the consequences of hardening my heart, and I didn't want to grow bitter and resentful, judgmental and critical. I didn't want to get stuck in emotional quicksand. I had lived too much life and gotten unstuck from too many past places to forfeit my future and all that God wanted to continue doing in and through me. I had come too far, gained too much ground in my heart, to give it all up now.

So, like I had so many times before, I sought to sort out all my feelings and the facts I understood. I knew I had to navigate them in a healthy way so my emotions didn't cloud what I knew to be truth—about God, about myself, about my friend.

But I must admit, I have the capacity to overthink obsessively, and trying to figure out what went wrong consumed me. In my book *Unashamed*, I described that one of my greatest strengths—*and* weaknesses—is my ability to analyze everything. Like most people, I find it difficult to trust God when I do not understand what is happening. But trying to reason through the unreasonable only leads me into an endless loop of mental searching that leads nowhere—and this time was no different. I spent weeks analyzing every conversation, rereading every text, rehashing every time we were together, trying desperately to figure out what I had done to deserve this. If you're an obsessive analyzer like me, then you know as well as I do, it doesn't solve anything.

I also knew from all I had walked through in life that when I feel something so deeply, I shouldn't do what many of us are tempted to do, and what I often had done in my past. I should not try to run from the pain by burying myself in my work. I shouldn't try to numb the pain by ignoring the entire situation, acting as though nothing had happened, as though I didn't care. I did care—deeply. I knew that I needed to deal with it, work *through* it, and not let it derail me.

My life and ministry are built on relationships. Everything I do is all about trying to connect people to God and to help them love each other. The enemy would have loved for me to harden my heart, shut down, and withdraw from any genuine friendships. He tried to convince me that life is easier if we keep people at a distance, erect a wall around our heart, and prevent people from getting in too close. Even though I had many thriving friendships, this pain was taking all my focus, and I *almost* believed the lie of the enemy: that pursuing true, intimate, godly friendships was just too hard at my age and stage in life.

I knew I needed to start with forgiving. After all, that is what I spend my life teaching others to do. But it is never as easy as it sounds, especially when our heart is broken. I knew I couldn't let what happened to me become what I believed about myself. Just because someone hurt me didn't mean I was unworthy, unlovable, or unkind. It didn't mean I was worth less or worthless. It didn't mean I was not a good friend or capable of being a good friend. But that's how I felt—no matter how many times I tried to refute all the lies bombarding my mind. *If I were a good friend to her, she wouldn't have cut me off without an explanation. If I were a good friend to her, she would hear me out and make time for me. If I were a good friend to her . . .*

But I *had* been a good friend to her. I had done the best I knew. And regardless of what I might have done wrong, I truly loved her and wanted the best for her. I wanted our friendship to last. I never imagined it ending—especially not like this.

If I were going to move beyond this pain and not get stuck

in this one dark moment of my life, I knew I had to quit obsessing over past events and fall into the arms of God, letting him help me sort through all my emotions—and get control of my runaway-train thoughts.[1]

When I reached out to my friend to talk and find a resolve, it was to no avail. She didn't want to talk it through with me any more than it seemed Sophia's friends wanted to talk to her. She had simply shut down, and shut me out.

INVITE JESUS IN

None of us starts out in life planning to be hurt—or to hurt others—but it happens. People fail us—and we fail people—repeatedly. It happens in our childhood and continues all the way through our adulthood. Our lives are intertwined with everyone around us—just as God designed—but we are all a part of a flawed humanity. None of us ever arrives, so it stands to reason that every time we open our hearts to one another, every time we're thrown together into each other's worlds, we will, quite possibly, hurt one another.

Whether it occurs in our dating, marriage, work, or friendships, it is going to happen. I've heard so many stories from women who started out their careers full of enthusiasm and talent only to be devastated by life-altering criticism that postponed or derailed their success. They didn't know how *not* to believe everything someone in a position of authority said and how *not* to let it define who they were. So they minimized their talent and settled for a less fulfilling position. They believed the lies that they were not smart enough, not gifted enough, not savvy enough.

I've listened to stories from women who married the love of their life only to have the marriage eventually crumble. Because of all the hurtful words thrown at them, they believed they were a failure and that they were unworthy of a loving relationship.

Just because we experience failure, it doesn't make us a failure—but that's hard to process when we don't know how.

My own aunt was married for twenty-five years when she learned her best friend had been having an affair with her husband for eighteen of those years. She was devastated, and it was so hard watching her internalize lies about herself because of their deceitful actions. She agonized over not understanding how she never knew. She questioned everything she'd ever done or said that might have made both of them betray her. She obsessed over what she could have done differently, believing she was the one who had failed.

We have all been through deeply painful situations where words or actions significantly wounded us and threatened to derail us—whether it was from a friend, a spouse, a colleague, or a mentor. When we were . . .

- Blindsided by a divorce
- Upstaged by a coworker
- Shamed publicly by a leader
- Financially ruined by a business partner
- Judged by a family member
- Rejected by a lifelong friend
- Betrayed by a ministry partner

We've never forgotten those times when we lost our peace, joy, and hope and sometimes our vision, passion, and purpose.

Unexpected emotional wounding is so deeply painful because it is . . . unexpected. It hits when our defenses are down and our trust levels are up. How critical then to understand that even when people leave us and hurt us, God never leaves us nor forsakes us.[2] He understands what it feels like to be kicked in the gut, to have the wind knocked out of us—and he cares. He promises to be there for us and to help us. "If your heart is broken," writes the psalmist, "you'll find God right there; if you're kicked in the gut, he'll help you catch your breath" (Psalm 34:18 MSG). Even when people are unfaithful, God is always faithful.

Every time we're deeply hurt, we're faced with the opportunity to let that wound define us—for a season or for the rest of our lives. Maybe we've altered our course, scaled back our dreams, or given up on them all together. Maybe we've believed something about ourselves—consciously or subconsciously—that may not be true. That's what I had faced more than once—and that's what Sophia was grappling with that unforgettable night.

REFRAME YOUR QUESTION

I remember when the initial shock of my friend hurting me began to subside, and I slowly realized that I had to work through all my hurt without her. It was a defining moment in my healing, a moment of reckoning, of turning my attention from how deeply hurt I felt to how I could get better. But I really wasn't sure I could do it alone—and be as healthy as I wanted to be—and so I decided to get help.

When we get a hit out of nowhere that threatens to knock

us out, we need wise Christian counsel. I'm a big believer in going to Jesus and to safe people who can help us process unexpected wounds. Because of my past wounds—like those from my childhood—I knew I was vulnerable in this area, so I reached out to a Christian counselor who could help me. I knew that ultimately Jesus is the only one who can truly heal our deepest hurts, but I also knew the value of having someone help me sort out my perspectives and my heart.

Unexpected hurts often reveal unexpected pain, and, as strange as it may sound, I wanted to take advantage of this opportunity to be healed of anything lurking under the surface of which I might not have been aware. I've been on this journey long enough now to know that when I feel a certain type of heart pain, it is an invitation from God for a deeper healing he wants to do in me. I have been so broken, wounded, and fragmented that I am a constant work in progress. I've learned to lean into this kind of pain when it happens—even though I know that doing so will hurt—because I so desperately desire the healing I know is on the other side.

I know that God sometimes uses relational fractures to show us where we are out of alignment with him; maybe our affections are misplaced. It's so easy to have unrealistic expectations of others—to inadvertently want them to love us as only God can—and to set our friendships up for failure. We can't expect people to be Jesus to us. It's too unfair. Jesus is the only true friend who can love us unconditionally and really stick closer than a brother.[3]

So, it was then, with a counselor's help, that I slowly quit asking, *Why, God, why?*—because honestly, sometimes we may never know, and because that question usually just spirals us into a dark hole that leads nowhere. Instead I started asking,

Jesus, where are you in this? What can you show me through this? What can I learn from this?

It wasn't the first time I'd been unexpectedly hurt, so I knew there was always *something* God wanted to do in me. He didn't cause the hurt—my friend did—but God is always eager to use our circumstances to bring more wholeness into our lives, if we will let him. God is good; God does good; and God uses all things for my good.[4] These are truths I believe with all my heart. So, as I invited him in, I knew he would use this for my good somehow.

Reframing my questions changed my perspective. It turned my focus back toward Jesus—where real answers come from. It reconnected me to hope—which meant I was looking forward now and not backward at all the emotional wreckage in my wake. It also set my heart in a direction of letting Jesus mold me further into being the kind of friend I had always wanted.

Only Jesus could heal me completely, so I took the time to tell Jesus of the loss I felt—like part of my life was missing—and he walked me through the sorrow of how much all of this had hurt me. I grieved the loss of someone I had come to love dearly. I grieved the loss of not having to second-guess my words or filter my responses. I grieved the loss of having a friend who understood me implicitly and let me be myself. I missed all the time and space she filled in my life. I missed all the laughter we shared. I missed all the deep conversations we used to have. I missed the random texts and jokes and prayer requests. And I told him all of this. I allowed myself to be in touch with how I truly felt by being honest with God and myself. And as I did my part, God began to do what only he could do—heal my heart.

FORGIVE FREELY

Jesus completely forgives us every single time we make a mistake, and he wants us to freely give that same gift to others. He wants us to forgive every offense—no matter how big or how small. Sometimes, when the hurt is deep, it can take longer to heal, and the relationship may never go back to how it was before. In fact, God may not even want that. But there can be peace and grace-giving communication between us. Jesus wants us to practice love, grace, and mercy—especially with those who wound us most, because they are often the most wounded.

I have discovered that when I hurt people (and I am devastated by my capacity to wound), it is often because of a broken place in me—a place of ignorance, fear, insecurity, or jealousy I didn't realize was there. I'm so grateful for the friends who extend grace, love, and forgiveness to me. I'm so thankful for the ones who love me enough to keep walking beside me, despite my shortcomings.

In other situations, when I felt like someone had hurt me in a manner that was illogical or irrational, I would often learn later that they had been going through their own pain, or had a wound from their past that was affecting our friendship. It always explained so much. When I realized their pain, I could truly understand and be more understanding. Revelations like that always turned my inwardly fixated thoughts to outwardly focused compassion for what they must be feeling, and allowed me to extend grace toward them.

Each time I've been unexpectedly hurt, it has renewed my resolve to be quicker to ask for forgiveness—so I practice ongoing forgiveness as often as possible. As a wife, I can lapse in kindness or attention. Sometimes, my fiery Greek emotions get the best of me, and I say things that are unfair. When I realize how I've sounded or what I've done, I ask Nick to forgive me. As a mother, I get plenty of opportunities as well. I love my girls with all my heart, but I don't always get it right, so I ask them to forgive me. I'm a strong woman with convictions and visions and dreams for the future, so as a leader with more than two hundred members on our team, I don't always get it right there either. In those times when I realize I've blown it, I want mercy. No matter the difference of opinion, or the differences in personality and interpretation of the circumstances, I want forgiveness and grace.

That's what Jesus was wanting his disciples—and us—to understand when he responded to Peter's question: "'Lord, how many times shall I forgive my brother or sister who sins against me? Up to seven times?' Jesus answered, 'I tell you, not seven times, but seventy-seven times'" (Matthew 18:21–22).

I find it significant that, of all the disciples who could have asked Jesus about forgiveness, it was Peter who posed this question. It wasn't long afterward that Peter had to practice an even more difficult kind of forgiveness—he had to forgive himself.

It happened the night of the Last Supper, when Jesus and the disciples left the upper room after their Passover meal and walked to the Mount of Olives. Jesus began to speak, and he prophesied that some of them would fall away. It was Peter who quickly spoke up declaring his devotion: "Even if all fall away on account of you, I never will" (Matthew 26:33).

"Truly I tell you," Jesus answered, "this very night, before the rooster crows, you will disown me three times" (verse 34).

But Peter was persistent: "'Even if I have to die with you, I will never disown you.' And all the other disciples said the same" (verse 35).

Jesus then invited his disciples to go with him to the garden of Gethsemane. There, he invited Peter and the two sons of Zebedee to come closer, as he poured out his grief. And he asked them, "Sit here while I go over there and pray" (verse 36).

When he returned an hour later, he found them sleeping, and he said to Peter, "Couldn't you men keep watch with me for one hour? . . . Watch and pray so that you will not fall into temptation. The spirit is willing, but the flesh is weak" (verses 40–41).

Jesus went away again to pray a second time, and then a third, and each time returned to find them sleeping. It was after the third time that he woke them up, telling them that his betrayer, Judas, had come—and he came accompanied by a crowd carrying swords and clubs.

The angry mob took Jesus to Caiaphas, the high priest, where teachers of the law and elders had assembled, and it was Peter who followed at a safe distance, eventually positioning himself in the courtyard where he could see and hear what was happening.

Now Peter was sitting out in the courtyard, and a servant girl came to him. "You also were with Jesus of Galilee," she said. But he denied it before them all. "I don't know what you're talking about," he said.

Then he went out to the gateway, where another servant girl saw him and said to the people there, "This fellow was with Jesus of Nazareth."

He denied it again, with an oath: "I don't know the man!"

After a little while, those standing there went up to Peter and said, "Surely you are one of them; your accent gives you away."

Then he began to call down curses, and he swore to them, "I don't know the man!"

Immediately a rooster crowed. Then Peter remembered the word Jesus had spoken: "Before the rooster crows, you will disown me three times." And he went outside and wept bitterly.

MATTHEW 26:69–75

Peter was heartbroken over his own human frailty. He had fallen asleep earlier in the garden when Jesus asked them to pray—more than once—and now he had denied even knowing Jesus three times. He had been fearful for his own life, fearful to be discovered as one of Jesus's disciples, but when he realized all he had done, how he had denied a cherished friend, the true Messiah, someone he loved, his heart was shattered.

How many times have we been the one who wounded someone else? How many times have we wished we could wind back time and have a do-over? Whether we are the ones who are wounded, or the ones inflicting the pain, our hearts can be just as broken and just as in need of healing.

When Peter realized what he had done, he was bitterly disappointed in himself. But despite his tragic failure, Peter went on to fulfill his destiny, just as Jesus had said: "And I tell you, you are Peter, and on this rock I will build my church, and the gates of hell shall not prevail against it" (Matthew 16:18 ESV). God used Peter despite his human imperfections and failings. And through Peter's ministry, the door of the church was opened to the Jews, the Samaritans, and the Gentiles— virtually the entire world at that time.[5]

But what if Peter had never forgiven himself? What if he'd kept his focus on himself and all his pain? Stuck in a moment. Imagine if he'd let his broken heart hold him back.

Forgiveness—freely asking for it from God and others,

freely offering it to those who hurt us, and even freely extending it to ourselves—is part of how we heal.

Imagine if I'd let my broken heart hold me back every time it has been broken. I certainly wouldn't have been whole enough to be the kind of mother Sophia needed that night when she poured out all her hurt to me. And in my marriage, I wouldn't be the kind of wife that I've learned to be. I would be making Nick pay for things he'd never done, because my actions toward him would all be rooted in past hurts and abuse inflicted by other people—some going all the way back to kindergarten.

Isn't that what we do when we have unresolved relational wounds? We carry them from one relationship to the next. A new boss shouldn't have to deal with all the wounds from a former boss who didn't know how to lead, guide, and coach us in a healthy manner. A new friend shouldn't have to be assessed based on how the last friend hurt us. A new spouse should never have to pay for what an ex-spouse did. But if we don't invite Jesus in to heal us from the wounds of past relationships, then that's exactly what will happen, whether we realize it or not. We'll hold back, fearful of opening up our hearts freely, unable to understand that just because someone in our past hurt us doesn't mean everyone in our future will.

BE OPEN TO UNEXPECTED BLESSINGS

I don't know your story, but I do understand that when we experience heartbreak, it can feel like our story is over, that we have reached a dead end. When people unexpectedly attack us, betray or reject us—overtly or subtly—our souls can become so discouraged that we're tempted to give up. But when we invite Jesus into our messy narrative, as we tell him about our story and about all our pain, then he can start reshaping our perspective, reviving our fragmented heart, and restoring our ability to feel, love, and care. As we invite him in, he can refill our heart with compassion—just as he did when he saved us— and we can begin to trust again.

Trusting again is the way God wants all our stories to unfold, because trust is the fuel that keeps us moving forward in faith, embracing all the unexpected adventure that he has planned for us. God created us to do life with people. And in order to fulfill our purpose, we will need to build and nurture relationships, connections that involve people who are very human and could quite possibly hurt us. We must learn how to guard our hearts, and yet, at the same time, be vulnerable to those we pull in close.

My friend, who I had pulled in so close, eventually did agree to talk heart to heart, and I learned she had been hurt in a separate situation and was so caught up in her pain and struggle that she didn't realize how much she hurt me. She was simply trying to survive in her own battles, and instead of drawing me in to fight alongside her, she pushed me away. I understood, and I forgave her, but it proved to be one more instance of how hurting people hurt people. If we are to have healthy relationships, then we need to learn how to be good at saying what Jesus said to those who crucified him: "Forgive them, for they know not what they do."[6]

I want to stay healthy, so I fully forgive others, and I keep putting myself out there, risking new relationships—even if it means I might get hurt. I do my best to share my friends' sad times as well as their happy times. I do my best to over-look offenses and to ask for forgiveness when I offend. I keep choosing to be vulnerable, to keep myself connected to people, because God created us to need each other, to love one another.

That was the divine tension Sophia faced. As we continued to talk in that season, she and her friends reunited, but a new dynamic grew among them. The next year, she went to a new school and learned some valuable lessons: *some friends are for a season; some friends are safe up close; and some are only safe from a distance.* We can't bring everyone into our inner circle and trust them equally. Because she learned not to define herself by how others treated her, or to shut off her heart because of unex-pected hurt but let it remain open for unexpected blessings in the future, she easily made new friends.

I was delighted one day when she asked if she could have a sleepover with a girl she had met and bonded with at school. Nick and I went upstairs and gave them free rein in the kitchen and TV room. They filled the entire evening with movies and loads of popcorn. Sitting in my room, I couldn't help but overhear their attempts at whispering that turned into hushed giggles and bursts of uncontrollable laughter. As the evening turned into night, it would have been useless to ask them to quiet down—but truthfully, I didn't want to. Catching snippets of their conversations every so often, I couldn't stop smiling. I was so happy she hadn't pulled back and missed the unexpected richness of a great new friendship.

Had her journey been painful? Yes. For her and for me.

Had it been worth it? Well, judging by the lack of sleep I got that night listening to all the giggles that never stopped, I think yes.

Chapter Five

WHEN THE UNEXPECTED DISILLUSIONS

Becoming a Prisoner of Hope

───

*We must accept finite disappointment,
but never lose infinite hope.*
—MARTIN LUTHER KING JR.

Y ou can get dressed now, LoriAnn."
Covered only by a light blanket and sheet, LoriAnn stirred slightly at the sound of the nurse's voice. Still foggy-headed from the waning sedative, she felt helpless to move, much less get up. The heaviness of her heart and all the years of struggle seemed to weigh her down, pinning her to the bed. Squinting against the harsh fluorescent lights, straining to focus, she tried to will her body into action, but all she could manage was to grasp the outer edge of the blanket.

Glancing at her surroundings, she noticed the curtain had been pulled aside, exposing the rest of the recovery room. It appeared as sterile and disappointing as her last sonogram. Where there should have been a bright, pulsing miracle of life, there had been only stillness. Instinctively, her hand went to her abdomen. The place her growing baby had been was now just a knot of grief and anxiety. She had loved him from the moment he was hoped for through all the time she carried him. Her heart had never quit beating for him—even when his gave out. She would never stop loving him. Never stop wanting to hold him.

"You can get up and get dressed when you're ready," the nurse repeated.

The groggy effects of the anesthesia were wearing off, but what remained pushed LoriAnn to a jagged edge.

And then what? Go home and pretend nothing ever happened? Go back to work and try to act like everything's normal? Nothing is normal. And nothing will ever be normal again. . . . All I wanted was a baby . . . my baby . . .

The nurse simply meant it as a kind prompt, but LoriAnn's frayed mind couldn't stop intensifying her broken heart and the harsh betrayal of her empty womb.

You can get dressed now because . . .

You will never be a mother.

You will never celebrate Mother's Day.

You are flawed. Broken. Ill-equipped. Irreparable.

And there's nothing you can do about any of it.

Rolling to her side and burying her face in the sheet, LoriAnn wanted to cry, wanted to feel the release, but she couldn't. The flare of anger had collapsed into feelings of nothingness and numbness—the calm that always preceded the storm she knew would come. She knew getting dressed wouldn't help anything. It wouldn't erase years of fading hopes. It wouldn't quench the longing in her soul. It wouldn't prepare her for the silence waiting at home. That's where the tears would come—in the profound sadness and loneliness waiting for her in the echoing quiet of her bedroom. No clothes would ever hide her shattered heart or cover all the shame she felt. Nothing was going to shield her from the insensitive things people would say, even if they meant well, especially when they offered, "Don't worry, you can always try again," or "Well, it's not like losing an actual child." *Yes, it was. It was exactly like losing my child.*

Too many times, those kinds of comments had seared her heart and left her doubled over inside. She had always managed to mumble some niceties, but this time, she knew she could never bear it again—because she could never try again. She had fought so hard to stay pregnant—every time she had been pregnant— but this time marked the end of a battle she no longer had the strength to fight. A battle that left her no choice but to surrender.

She knew the tsunami of emotions would come—as they had each time before. The grief that would evolve into rage, relentlessly crashing into her every waking thought and sleep-deprived dreams. The edge she would topple over every time she overheard women complain about being pregnant or about their children. The bitterness and resentment that would take up long-term occupancy in her heart and become so hard to evict.

It was so unfair. All she had ever wanted to be was a mother. From the time she played with dolls as a child to when she babysat as a teen, she imagined what it would be like to chase her own children throughout the house. The older she grew, whenever someone offered to let her hold a baby, she was already reaching for it, delighted to coo and cuddle. She found so much joy in hosting baby showers for her girlfriends, celebrating each of their newfound joys. When she married, she couldn't wait for the day when she would hold one of her own. It was just a matter of time.

But it never occurred to her that time wouldn't be able to give her what she wanted most.

Having a baby was the one thing LoriAnn had thought

every woman could do—and what she'd always believed God intended for her to do. When pregnancy after pregnancy failed, she began to pray like Sarah, like Hannah, like Elizabeth, like every woman called barren in the Bible. And even when she tried all the modern medical efforts those women never were afforded, she found herself in the same familiar place: letting go of what she wanted to hold onto the most.

I tried, LoriAnn silently screamed. *I tried so hard.*

Nothing was as she had envisioned it to be, as she had prayed it would be, as she had hoped it would be. And nothing could silence the never-ending cry of her heart for a child. The cycle of pregnancies unexpectedly ending in miscarriage after miscarriage had taken its toll. Her emotions and her marriage had worn thin, too thin. And now, hopelessness consumed her.

WHEN DREAMS DIE

Getting up and getting dressed that day began one of the hardest uphill climbs of LoriAnn's life, because that day left her grieving the future she would never have. That day left her feeling what we all can experience when our greatest hopes and biggest dreams die—when our lives are unexpectedly interrupted with a finality we couldn't have predicted or controlled. Whether our dream was wrapped up in a baby we wanted so badly, in a marriage that ended abruptly, a business venture that failed, a friendship that unraveled, a ministry that never flourished, or a job opportunity that fell through, in those shattered moments we can feel so forsaken and alone, helpless and held captive by despair. Feelings of hopelessness can leave us wanting to pull back and rewrite the rest of our lives as a smaller, safer story than the adventurous one God originally planned for us. It's so easy to grow afraid to hope again—especially in the area of our greatest disappointment.

When I first met LoriAnn, I never would have guessed the heartache she had lived through. I was hosting an A21 awareness trip in Thessaloniki, Greece, for a group of women from her church, and over a lunch of Greek salad with extra feta cheese, we clicked. She is Lebanese and Syrian, and with me being Greek, we joked that maybe it was because of our Mediterranean blood. It was fun to meet a woman who could talk as fast as me, was as passionate, driven, and focused as me, and gestured with her hands as much as I did.

One evening, at a tiny Greek restaurant, our dinner transitioned into a late-night conversation about everything, including all the loss she had endured and the despair she had felt. When she finished telling her story, I sat there stunned.

There was such pain in her eyes as she told me about finally accepting that the baby she had wanted most in her life could never be delivered into her arms. I recognized in her the same agonizing look I had seen before in the eyes of so many women—women who were desperate to have a child, who tried every possible procedure to do so. I couldn't imagine the hopelessness LoriAnn had known, living through such a cycle of suffering, and spending more than a decade desperately trying to carry a child to term. But here she was, somehow having found a way to trust God again after all her hope had been lost. I was captivated by her faith, and I wanted to know more.

Following the loss of her last pregnancy, when she realized she could never try again, she spent the next five years battling severe and unexpected health issues that required numerous surgeries followed by painful recoveries. And yet, even in the midst of her health challenges, she managed to advance to the top of her corporation, eventually occupying an office in Manhattan. When she was seemingly on top of the world professionally, the industry she had mastered began to crumble under an investigation by the attorney general. The fallout damaged major companies around the world, and LoriAnn was soon saying painful goodbyes to many colleagues who, through no fault of their own, had lost their jobs.

When it seemed she couldn't—and shouldn't—lose any more, she lost the one person she had trusted more than anyone. What had worn thin in her marriage finally snapped. Although she and her husband had enjoyed a strong partnership early on, all the losses over the years left deep scars on their relationship. Even the best of marriages can be broken when the volley of unexpected blows leaves no space or time to fully recover from each loss—and when one partner chooses to walk away from what both once valued and leaves no room for God to intervene or help the couple reconcile.

The month their marriage ended turned into the most devastating month of LoriAnn's life. The day her divorce was final, one of her best friends unexpectedly died. Two weeks later, her dad, the rock of her life, also passed away.

If ever there was someone who had good reason to give in to hopelessness and to give up on God, it was LoriAnn. Her life had literally unraveled—through miscarriages, health challenges, professional losses, divorce, and death. And yet here she was full of faith, having traveled to the other side of the world because she wanted to share in the work of the gospel, in a work that literally rescues exploited men, women, and children and gives them hope.

I knew from her story that it hadn't been easy to pull through the dark times. She told me how she had always been analytical, a planner, a list maker, and yet none of her preparations could stop any of the tragedies that happened one right after the other. At one point, after so much loss, she admitted she had felt resentment toward God. In her Christian walk, she had done all the right things, said all the right things, and participated in all the right things, and yet she still felt distant from God.

But that's when she chose to lean into him rather than walk away. As she drew near to him, he drew near to her.[1] I was so moved when she told me, "I knew that my God was a God of hope and a God of destiny. I knew enough to know that I could not let hopelessness be what destroyed me. I could not let my heart spiral out of control. I had to press in and trust him."

LoriAnn's description of her journey deeply resonated with what I knew to be true, that even the most hopeless situations do not have to be the end of everything. The end of a chapter—no matter how unexpected or tragic—doesn't have to be the end of our story. When all we feel is utter hopelessness, by faith we can still choose to believe that Jesus is the way, the truth, and the life—for us and for our family.[2] We can believe that Jesus has the power to recreate and redeem our lives no matter how much the destroyer has destroyed. By faith, we can lean into Jesus and risk hoping again, trusting that he will take us by the hand and lift us up, that our lives of ruin will be made whole, that our sorrows will be comforted.[3]

Sitting before me, LoriAnn struck me as a living example of words the prophet Zechariah had used thousands of years ago when he called the Israelites "prisoners of hope" (Zechariah 9:12). Instead of living in despair for the rest of her life—living but not really living, which would have been so easy to do—she had risked it all to hope again.

THE WAY FORWARD

For seventy years, the children of Israel had been held captive in Babylon while the enemy pillaged their homeland. When they at last returned home, they found nothing but destruction. Even Jerusalem and the temple had to be rebuilt. But in the midst of their despair, Zechariah—whose name means "The Lord has remembered"[4]—prophesied hope for their future:

> Rejoice greatly, O daughter of Zion! Shout aloud, O daughter of Jerusalem! Behold, your king is coming to you; righteous and having salvation is he, humble and mounted on a donkey, on a colt, the foal of a donkey.
>
> I will cut off the chariot from Ephraim and the war horse from Jerusalem; and the battle bow shall be cut off, and he shall speak peace to the nations; his rule shall be from sea to sea, and from the River to the ends of the earth.
>
> As for you also, because of the blood of my covenant with you, I will set your prisoners free from the waterless pit. *Return to your stronghold, O prisoners of hope; today I declare that I will restore to you double.*
>
> ZECHARIAH 9:9–12 ESV, emphasis added

The children of Israel had endured loss after loss, hardship after hardship, and all they could see across the landscape of their lives was more of the same, just as LoriAnn had experienced. Every dream, every hope, every future they had planned and built was gone, but God had not forgotten them.

God knew that the way for his people to escape their pit of despair—the same place of fear and hopelessness in which we all sometimes find ourselves—was for them to become prisoners of hope.

He knew that returning to their stronghold—their promised Messiah and king—was the answer. Risking hope in God again—even though their confidence had been shaken—was the way forward.

CHOOSE LOCK-DOWN

Hope is unshakeable confidence in God.[5] It doesn't deny the reality of our pain, but it does give us a life beyond our pain. It gives us permission to believe in a new beginning. It is the happy and confident expectation of good that lifts our spirits and dares us to believe for a different future. It is always looking to God with expectation: "But now, Lord, what do I look for? My hope is in you" (Psalm 39:7).

But when we lose hope, when all we feel is the pain of loss and disappointment, it can be so hard to believe that God wants to help us, or that he cares, because we have more questions than answers. More doubt than faith. And yet, that is the perfect time to become a prisoner of hope.

A prisoner of hope sounds like an odd thing to be, doesn't it? Aren't prisoners locked up in high-security institutions and stripped of all their freedoms? Why would we want to be characterized as a prisoner of anything, even hope?

Because being a prisoner of hope in God is different. God's prisoners of hope aren't forced into an institution for punishment but invited into a fortress for safety. Imagine a castle that stands firm even when the very foundations of life are shaken. A place created just for us, where we can chain ourselves to the promise that God is working all things for our good, even when all things are falling apart. From the high tower of this fortress, we prisoners of hope gain a whole new perspective.

We can look beyond our unexpected circumstances to the future, trusting that God has good things in store for us.

When I first learned to think and live this way, it was revolutionary to me. I was raised in a religious tradition that never encouraged me to expect good things from God. In fact, it was considered presumptuous to even imagine that God had time for my requests, given that he had an entire world to run. I'm so glad I discovered in his Word that God is good, God does good, and God wants to do good for me—all the time. But to keep my heart and mind thinking and believing this way on a daily basis doesn't come naturally; instead, it's always a choice, one I have to make again and again.

Here's another way to think about this choice. When the unexpected strikes, we find ourselves perched on a thin precipice with an abyss on either side. That's when we have a decision to make. We can choose to fall into the abyss of despair on one side, or into the abyss of hope on the other. Both look like scary choices, but when we choose to fall into hope we soon find ourselves wrapped in the arms of a loving God—a God who always catches us and always promises to carry us from the precipice of despair into the wide-open space of new life. That's where we find the new opportunities and experiences that get us beyond our disappointments and disillusionments. It is a place of freedom where we let go of what we once wanted in exchange for what we never expected—a new adventure. But we can't get there by ourselves. Only God can catch and carry us into the new life we never imagined and take us to places we never considered going.

Becoming a prisoner of hope doesn't mean we no longer struggle with disillusionment or despair. When the unexpected strikes and gives us new reasons to lose hope, it's still tempting to dig a tunnel out of our fortress, to escape hope and lose ourselves in doubt, fear, and unbelief. I cannot tell you how many times I almost lost hope that we would see people rescued at A21, or that traffickers would be caught and prosecuted and sentenced. That Propel would resonate with women. That I had another book in me, or for that matter that I even would finish this one. There were times I wondered if I would have the ability to parent my girls with wisdom. Or if I would get free from the pain of my past. The list is endless.

In each and every endeavor, I had to chain myself once more to the God of all hope. As we launched our ministry initiatives, people who said they would stay, left. People who were supportive at one stage dropped out in the next. Doors slammed shut. Governments changed policies. But I have learned to walk by faith and not by sight. To close my eyes, proclaim myself a prisoner of hope, and step into a spiritual fortress—to dare to get my hopes up and keep my hopes up. I've seen God step in and carry me to better places, present me with better opportunities, and lead me into amazing breakthroughs.

When we are tempted to escape but choose instead to run into our stronghold Jesus, he promises to overflow our lives with hope: "May the God of hope fill you with all joy and peace as you trust in him, so that you may overflow with hope by the power of the Holy Spirit" (Romans 15:13). He promises to help us become the prisoners of hope he's called us to be so we can move beyond despair into a new destiny.

But first, just as LoriAnn did, we have to willingly turn ourselves in at the fortress gate and stay there. When she said she knew God was a God of hope, and that she had to press in and trust him, LoriAnn was making that choice. She was choosing to hope when there was no logical reason to hope, and when everything around her was screaming at her to choose otherwise. LoriAnn's feelings of hopelessness were valid and painfully real, but by faith she chose to become a prisoner of hope and, as strange as it sounds, that's where she found her true freedom. That's where she found her wide-open spaces—and it's where we will find ours.

GIVE HOPE A VOICE

Turning ourselves in as prisoners of hope begins with a decision, but learning how to stay within God's fortress of safety every single day of our lives is a process. Remember when I learned that I had cancer and I encamped myself in a "faith cocoon"—staying diligent in the Word, listening to worship music continuously, and only allowing faith-filled voices to speak into my life? That's how I kept myself within the fortress of God's love and care. Within those walls, anchored to God's promises, I could stay in faith and keep the fear of what cancer could do to me from gripping my heart.

That's how we become prisoners of hope. We lock ourselves down in God's promise of a future. We risk full confidence in him and his plan for our lives, even though nothing has turned out like we thought it would.[6] We find fellow prisoners who will be our friends and encourage our faith. We saturate ourselves in worship, declaring the truth of who God is as we fix our eyes on him in expectation. We believe the truth of God's Word over the facts of our circumstances. We act a lot like a young boy named David who did the "impossible" when he killed a giant named Goliath—with nothing more than a slingshot and five smooth stones. Do you remember the story?

Goliath showed up to the fight with just the facts of the circumstances:

> He looked David over and saw that he was little more than a boy, glowing with health and handsome, and he despised him. He said to David, "Am I a dog, that you come at me with sticks?" And the Philistine cursed David by his gods. "Come here," he said, "and I'll give your flesh to the birds and the wild animals!"
>
> 1 SAMUEL 17:42–44

But David showed up with the truth:

> "You come against me with sword and spear and javelin, but I come against you in the name of the LORD Almighty, the God of the armies of Israel, whom you have defied. This day the LORD will deliver you into my hands, and I'll strike you down and cut off your head. This very day I will give the carcasses of the Philistine army to the birds and the wild animals, and the whole world will know that there is a God in Israel."
>
> 1 SAMUEL 17:45–46

David defeated the giant because he believed the Word of the Lord over Goliath's intimidating taunts. He understood what God wants us to understand: *The facts can change, but the truth never does.* The truth alone has the power to help us move from the hopelessness of what *is* to hope of what *will be*.

When we choose to become prisoners of hope, we don't exchange freedom for confinement; we exchange one prison for another. We exchange living in a prison of our own hopeless thoughts for a prison built on the truth of God's Word. Within that strong fortress, we anchor ourselves in the high tower of God's perspective on our future. Whenever I've felt tempted to despair, to flee my prison of hope, I've read and prayed verses that steadied me and quieted the fearful thoughts swirling around me. We may never be able to completely silence hopeless thoughts, but we can quiet them with truth. We quiet them when we read, believe, and pray the words of Jesus. We quiet them when we listen to God's voice in Scripture more than the voices of the past, the voices of social media, the voices of other people, or even the voices of our own thoughts.

Staying secured within the fortress walls of hope means taking captive every hopeless thought before it takes us captive:

> The weapons we fight with are not the weapons of the world. On the contrary, they have divine power to demolish strongholds. We demolish arguments and every pretension that sets itself up against the knowledge of God, and we take captive every thought to make it obedient to Christ.
>
> 2 CORINTHIANS 10:4–5

I know that taking captive every thought often requires a ruthless fight, and that sometimes it's a minute-by-minute battle. I have often said I am only one thought away from being overtaken by all I have been freed from. But I daily choose to be a prisoner of hope. I do this by giving hope a voice—in what I think and in what I say.

The voice of hope doesn't speak despair and anxiety—even though that might sometimes be all we feel. It doesn't sigh in resignation or declare the futility of a situation. It doesn't speak words of apathy or negativity. It doesn't use social media to post what's on our mind when whatever that is doesn't agree with what's on God's mind. When we give hope a voice, we discipline our minds to think what God thinks and to say what God says—and nothing else.

"Do not be anxious," Jesus said. But look at the connection he then makes between anxiety and how we use our words. "Do not be anxious, saying, 'What shall we eat?' or 'What shall we drink?' or 'What shall we wear?' . . . But seek first the kingdom of God" (Matthew 6:31–33 ESV).

Do not be anxious, saying . . .

We all feel anxious from time to time, but we don't have to talk up all the anxiety we're feeling. We don't have to magnify our anxious thoughts with our words. Instead, we can choose thoughts full of hope and faith and peace—and speak those. We can take counsel from the apostle Paul:

> Finally, brethren, whatsoever things are true, whatsoever things are honest, whatsoever things are just, whatsoever things are pure, whatsoever things are lovely, whatsoever things are of good report; if there be any virtue, and if there be any praise, think on these things.
>
> PHILIPPIANS 4:8 KJV

What if we used Paul's list of words as a filter for what we post on social media? As a filter for every family discussion, for every work meeting, for every phone call with a friend? Can you imagine how that would change the atmosphere and redirect every conversation toward hope? So many times when my thoughts wanted me to talk up anxiety or magnify disappointment, I have chosen instead to speak words of hope and faith and peace—and eventually that became what I felt. I marched my thoughts into God's strong fortress so I could continue living as a prisoner of hope.

Just as LoriAnn did, I've had many unexpected things happen in my life—things that were never in my plan. But in the same way LoriAnn's radiance and hope were a testimony to me, there is no telling what hope we can bring into our homes, workplaces, and communities, if we'll choose to be people of hope—who use words of hope—in a world where people desperately need it. That's why LoriAnn had come to Greece to learn about A21—because she knew firsthand the power of hope to resurrect a life. She knew that as the people of God, we never have to lose hope, even in the most hopeless situations. She knew that the same Spirit that raised Jesus from the dead lived in her—and in every believer on earth—and that he has the power to resurrect new life from the ashes of suffering and pain. "If the Spirit of him who raised Jesus from the dead is living in you," writes the apostle Paul, "he who raised Christ from the dead will also give life to your mortal bodies because of his Spirit who lives in you" (Romans 8:11). That's a promise of hope that will not fail.

HOPE IS AN ACT OF DEFIANCE

I don't know where your hope is struggling. Maybe your beleaguered hope is for . . .

- A loved one to be saved
- A child to come home
- A marriage to be restored

- Your body to be healed
- Your finances to be restored
- Your career to be revived
- A home of your own

Whatever it is, it's time to risk hoping again. Whatever dream we had that died, whatever promise we gave up on, the truth of God's Word says that we serve a God with resurrection power who specializes in raising the dead.[7] The truth we believe says we serve a God who redeems our lives from the pit, who gives us peace instead of conflict, who gives us a crown of beauty instead of ashes, who gives us the oil of joy instead of mourning, who gives us health instead of disease, liberty instead of captivity, assurance instead of doubt, hope instead of hopelessness.[8]

Our God is a transformational God. He transforms us from the inside out, and makes all things new in our lives—first in our spirits when we accept him as our Lord and Savior, and then in our souls as we continue to surrender areas of our lives to him:

> Therefore, if anyone is in Christ, he is a new creation. The old has passed away; behold, the new has come. . . . For our sake he made him to be sin who knew no sin, so that in him we might become the righteousness of God.
> 2 CORINTHIANS 5:17, 21 ESV

God is a God of redemption, restoration, and new beginnings. He's made you a new creation, and that newness can work from the inside out to change your today into a better tomorrow. If you don't like where you are right now, you don't have to settle or resign yourself to it. You can hold onto his promise as the truth that triumphs over the facts in your life: "He who began a good work in you will carry it on to completion until the day of Christ Jesus" (Philippians 1:6).

When we risk hoping again, we learn how to live in the present, but with the future in mind. We shift the gaze of our focus forward. We become prisoners of hope who cling to hope, who speak the language of hope, who don't put off hope, who are willing to let God surprise us with a new future. When we become prisoners of hope, we commit a daring act of defiance—we dare to get our hopes up. We dare to believe that the desires God has placed in our hearts will be fulfilled—somehow and some way.[9]

Will they look like we first imagined? Probably not.

Will we go through more disappointments? Most likely.

Will any of our future dreams die as well before they come to life? Quite possibly.

Why? Because every promise is tested. Every dream is challenged. God does not always do what we want, when we want, or how we want—but he is always ready to do exceedingly, abundantly, above and beyond anything we could ever ask or think.[10] He who promised really is faithful, no matter what it looks like in any season of our lives. When we become prisoners of hope, we declare with defiance that there is . . .

- No need God cannot meet
- No mountain God cannot move
- No prayer God cannot answer
- No sickness God cannot heal
- No heart God cannot mend
- No door God cannot open

When we become prisoners of hope, we aren't dismayed when dreams . . .

- Take longer than we think they should
- Cost more than we think they should
- Are harder to realize than we think they should be

When we become prisoners of hope, we shift our perspective. We . . .

- Look at what we have left, not what we have lost
- Believe the best, not assume the worst
- Keep moving forward, not shrink backward

It's time to become prisoners of hope, brave souls who are defiant in hope, who dare to get our hopes up. Let's refuse to throw away our confidence and trust in God, daring to believe he will reward our faith.

GOD RESTORES IN UNEXPECTED WAYS

When we risk becoming prisoners of hope, God can and will change what needs to be changed. We can get well. We can climb out of debt. We can forgive. We can be healed. We can overcome grief and loss—even the loss of a child. Losing a child at any stage of life is unimaginable pain and utterly devastating, and no child can ever be replaced, ever, but God can take us to a place where we no longer ache with our loss every moment of every day. If we lean into him, if we risk hoping and trusting him again, he can move us from our place of pain into a wide and spacious place of purpose. He can move us into a destiny we never might have considered. That's exactly what he did for LoriAnn.

Years after her miscarriages, God moved LoriAnn to a place where she became a mother to many. First, she became a stepmother to three children—including one she was blessed to mother from the time he was young. She was invited to join the board of one of the largest child abuse prevention organizations in the US, and served in that role for years. And she leads with Nick and me on the board of A21. God has made her maternal reach global—one in which her work benefits thousands upon thousands of children who have no mother to look after them. To her, that is the miracle God performed in her life, the double blessing Zechariah prophesied: "Return to your stronghold, O prisoners of hope; today I declare that I will restore to you double" (Zechariah 9:12 ESV).

"God healed my womb," LoriAnn told me after coming onto our board, "and I have become a mother to nations, something he put in my heart as a young girl."

Sometimes God gives us a revelation instead of a reason when he answers our prayers in unexpected ways. LoriAnn may never understand why she couldn't have her own children, but the call of God on her life to mother children still came to pass—and so did the fulfillment she longed for.

"He has used me because of my story," she said, "and not disqualified me because of what I have lived through." God is never finished with us—and whether we've gone through a divorce, suffered unimaginable hurts and losses, miscarriages in any area of our lives, he never sets us aside if we'll keep moving forward with him. If we'll keep putting our hope in him.

"But I had to learn a hard truth," LoriAnn added. "God fulfills what he puts in our hearts in unexpected ways. I had to learn that there are different ways I can mother. I can nurture and mentor young people. I can influence them and give them room in my heart. I can serve on boards that allow me to mother the motherless, to protect and shelter and defend the defenseless. It's so restorative to me to fight on behalf of women and children who can't fight for themselves. Isn't that what a mother does? A mother who wants the best for her children?"

Yes, it is.

Not long ago, LoriAnn returned from a trip to Thailand with our A21 team where she saw firsthand the horrors of how children are exploited there. I met her for lunch to hear about her trip, and brought my girls along. As we were catching up, she said to me so tenderly and sincerely, "Thank you for sharing your girls with me." I was moved. Catherine and Sophia are the joys of my life, but to realize how sharing them could bring someone else such joy touched me deeply. To let her—and other women in my life—help me mother my girls is a privilege, especially with someone who has so much to give, so much hope to offer.

Just as God did for LoriAnn, God wants to fulfill the dreams he's whispered to our hearts—no matter how long ago. We may have set them aside, but he's never forgotten even one of them. Let's dare to open our hearts and minds and allow God to revive our hopes. Let's risk giving him room to fulfill his plans and purposes for our lives in unexpected ways.

Chapter Six

WHEN THE UNEXPECTED DISHEARTENS

Living Wholeheartedly

Odd, how life makes twists and turns. I never would have guessed that I'd end up where I am now, but I wouldn't trade it for the world. I wouldn't trade this path I'm on for the whole solar system, for that matter. If I've learned anything these last several months, it's that sometimes the most scenic roads in life are the detours you didn't mean to take.

—ANGELA BLOUNT

You said we would only live here two years. Two years! Then it was another two years! And I was patient. I understood the reasons. But then it was another two on top of that. That's eight years, Sam! Eight years of waiting to move on with our lives. I'm sick of you saying, 'Just two more years.' I can't keep living like this—feeling like our lives are so temporary. We have three children now. We need stability. We need roots. Enough is enough!"

Kylie stared out the window remembering every harsh word she'd hurled at her husband the night before. Not one to cry, she couldn't suppress how painfully the words seared her heart—probably just like they must have stung Sam.

He's so tired of hearing me complain, she thought. *Heck, I'm tired of hearing me complain. But we can't keep living like this. I can't keep living like this.*

Although Kylie had taken out her frustrations and disappointment on her husband, she knew in her heart he wasn't the true cause of her misery. This was all about her. There was something God wanted to do inside of her. This whole chapter of her life had been so unexpected—so not what she had dreamed, so not what she thought marriage and ministry would be like—and she had not adjusted well.

Lord, I give up. Show me what to do. Help me change. Help me trust you.

Kylie had never really had to adapt to new surroundings. She had always lived a life of doing what was expected, living in a location that was expected, going to school as expected, attending church as expected. Even her circle of friends was expected. More than twenty-five years ago, she and I had been church friends who became best friends. We played squash together, dreamed about the future together, and couldn't wait to share Jesus with everyone we met. But unlike my life, Kylie's had been very predictable.

Where I had to overcome so many things—being abandoned, adopted, abused—she had been raised in a good Christian home with plenty of stability. Nothing in life had ever really rocked her internally. Nothing challenged the strength of her heart—until she married and moved away from everything she'd ever known.

Her family.

Her friends.

Her security.

Her identity.

That last one was the one that hurt the most. Deep down, she knew that was the real issue. She loved the strong sense of identity she'd had in her early years. She loved having so many friends, feeling like she lived in a world where she knew everyone and everyone knew her. She loved feeling together and in control. She loved the big city she lived in and all the perks of big city life. But all of that was what she left behind when she'd married and then moved to a small town eight years ago.

Things were hard from the very beginning. Kylie came to me that first year she and Sam were married and told me she wanted out of her marriage and out of the church. In fact, she wanted out of everything except her relationship with God. She still wanted to hang on to him.

When we feel like Kylie—when we believe God is our rock but the ground is shifting beneath our feet—it's tempting to look for an escape. Times of transition and change are almost always challenging, but especially so if it's the first time we've experienced a major upheaval. That's when our trust in God is severely tested.

I wasn't alarmed at Kylie's desperation, because I knew how much she loved God—and her husband. I realized she was upset because she felt like there was no road map for this leg of her journey, and she had never known such feelings of confusion and insecurity. As I listened to her and the Holy Spirit, I encouraged her to stay where God had placed her. I encouraged her to give it all to God and trust him, and she did. I knew there was something he wanted to do in *her*, even if neither of us knew exactly what that was right then.

For the next eight years, Kylie stayed in a place where

she felt she didn't fit in, a place she thought was temporary. She kept her heart distanced from people in the community because she thought they weren't planning to stay there long. Two years. Sam had promised. And every two years turned into two more. When the calendar rolled around to eight years, she succumbed to an avalanche of brokenheartedness. This *wasn't* temporary, and she knew something had to change. As hard as it was to admit, she was beginning to realize that the *something* was her own heart.

Every time we're faced with the unexpected, we have the choice to embrace it wholeheartedly or halfheartedly. Embracing it wholeheartedly keeps us moving forward in life; embracing it halfheartedly keeps us from growing. That's the truth Kylie was beginning to grasp.

"Moving from a big city to a rural area was a big adjustment," Kylie said. "I had always been ambitious. I grew up in a family that worked hard to achieve—whether that was an education, a nice house, extra money to go on trips or buy nice things. It was all I knew. I had grown up rewarding myself with a new purse, a new outfit, or a nice dinner out. When Sam took a position at a small church in a small town, I suddenly felt so out of place. There weren't options for shopping and dining out. And on our income, there was no room in the budget for anything extra.

"I felt odd around the other women in our community—like our values and interests were completely different. I especially felt like I had to hide my ambitions and career goals. I even downplayed my interests in nutrition and fitness because no one around me seemed to share those ideals. I felt that I had to hide these facets of my life because I was in a place where they weren't understood or accepted. I felt like an alien."

From Kylie's perspective, it seemed like the women in the community where she'd moved felt fulfilled once they were married and had kids. But Kylie's aspirations included a family *and* a career. This caused her to feel disconnected from the other women she met.

"To be honest, I didn't try to understand the women in the community where we'd moved," Kylie admitted. "I had no idea how to adjust to a place that felt like a wilderness. My heart just wasn't in it." Indeed, Kylie was *half*hearted.

Halfheartedness always has spiritual consequences. "I felt like I hadn't heard from God in years," Kylie said. "And I had been the young woman in youth group who was always so on fire for Jesus, who always felt like God was speaking to me. And now, there was just silence, loneliness, and disappointment. I showed up everywhere with a smile on my face because I was a 'good Christian,' but after eight years, my façade was wearing thin. I remember saying to Sam that night I vented my frustrations, 'I can't keep living in the wilderness!'"

LIVING WHOLEHEARTEDLY

Kylie's heart had been halved, broken in two by disappointment and fractured by her unwillingness to wholeheartedly embrace her unexpected. The only way for her to heal and move forward was to "whole" and strengthen her heart—to increase her heart's capacity to hope and believe. While she didn't really know how to do this, she knew enough to take the next step God showed her—something that began to move her in the direction of embracing her unexpected.

"To help make ends meet, I had been working full time,

but as we had our second and then our third child, we needed more money," Kylie said. "I remembered a message I had heard when I was young about doing what you can with what's in your hand. It was based on Ecclesiastes 9:10, 'Whatever your hand finds to do, do it with all your might.'

"So I asked the Lord, 'What's in my hand?' I pondered that question for days. *What's in my hand?* I loved fitness and I realized, *That's what's in my hand.* So I started my own business in health and fitness training.

"I don't know how I did it all back then—serving in church, running my own business, working my day job, and raising three kids. But I was learning something. I was learning who I was in God—my true identity. I needed to know who I was when I wasn't propped up by a title, prestige, close friends, new clothes, or family connections—all the things that once defined my life.

"I was so thankful that Sam heard my heart's cry and agreed to make changes," Kylie said. "We had been living in a rental house, always expecting that we might soon be moving, but that only fueled my sense of not belonging. So we decided to buy a house less than a mile from the church, which meant we could easily walk there. It may sound strange, but that kind of proximity made all the difference. It enabled me to get more involved in the community, and that helped me to begin really getting to know people. We were finally putting down roots. Our house was also across the street from a park, which meant the kids and I were there often and I had the opportunity to meet other moms. Now that I was connecting with others where I was, I found an unexpected grace waiting for me in this unexpected place. I was able to experience contentment. I was finally learning how to live and thrive in my wilderness."

The changes in lifestyle, culture, income, and stability were beyond difficult those first eight years—mostly because Kylie thought it would be temporary. She thought she was just passing through, on her way to somewhere else, and so she lived halfheartedly in her unexpected.

How many of us have been through something like that? We thought we were headed in one direction, only to look up a few years later and find ourselves unexpectedly lingering in a place we thought was short-term. A place we never counted on making permanent.

A job.

A town.

A circle of friends.

I can't help but compare this to the situation the children of Israel found themselves in after God freed them from four hundred years of slavery in Egypt. They thought they were embarking on a swift journey to their new forever home called the Promised Land. They had no intentions of living in tents in the desert for the next forty years.[1]

Tents. They had lived in houses all their lives. Sheltered. Protected. Inside those solid walls they'd practiced their faith, raised their families, celebrated births and marriages, and comforted one another in times of sorrow. But God led them into four decades of wilderness wandering—a temporary season—for a purpose.

God's first priority for us is always transformation—a change from the inside out. He almost always transforms *us* before he transforms our *circumstances*. When he led the children of Israel out of Egypt, he knew that he had to get "Egypt"—their old identity and slave mindset—out of them before they could truly enter the Promised Land. He had to transform them into conquerors who could go in and possess what he had promised. And it took forty years.[2]

When God led Kylie out of the big city—and away from all she had known—he knew her destiny. He knew her future. He knew her purpose and all her potential. And he knew the transformation she had to go through in order to be who she needed to be in the place he was preparing for her. God always prepares us for the place he has prepared for us. He wanted Kylie to learn how to strengthen her heart. He wanted her to learn how to move from halfhearted to wholehearted—a process that takes time and often unfolds in a wilderness. And he wanted her to learn how to apply what she learned to the rest of her life.

We all have wilderness seasons in our lives, times when everything that feels familiar, stable, and comforting falls away. But that's exactly why the wilderness is a place of transformation. With nothing to distract us from ourselves, and with no one but God to rely on, the conditions are ripe for growth and change. If we embrace the wilderness wholeheartedly, it becomes a place in which we are freed from our bondage to fear, insecurity, and disappointment. A place where we move from being self-absorbed to others-minded. A place where we quit trying to be self-sufficient and learn to be interdependent with one another and entirely dependent on God. It's where we learn to live wholehearted—to fully embrace the adventure that comes with the unexpected. The word *wholehearted* literally means "consecrated, dedicated, given over too fully, drenched."[3] That's the faith-filled mindset God wants to develop in us, and he uses every unexpected event in our lives to *whole* us, to heal our halved hearts and to help us grow.

For the children of Israel, those forty wilderness years were an unexpected delay, but they were also God's invitation to growth and transformation. Unfortunately, it was an invitation not all the people were willing to accept. In fact, virtually all of them actively resisted God's efforts to mature them, develop them, strengthen them, transform them, and to get them ready for the very thing they desired most of all—the Promised Land.

KEEP MOVING THROUGH

Out of the million or so men Moses led out of Egypt and across the desert, Caleb and Joshua were the only two who actually stepped foot across the Jordan River into the Promised Land.[4]

Just two. Out of a million.

Joshua and Caleb hung onto the promises of God through four wilderness decades, and now at last they were about to enter the land flowing with milk and honey.[5] They had lived in tents in the desert for forty long years, but they never forgot all that God had done for them and in them throughout the journey:

- God had parted the Red Sea so they could escape the Egyptian army, and then collapsed the sea to drown their pursuers.
- God fed them with manna, bread from heaven.
- God provided flocks of quail when they wanted meat, and water flowing from a rock when they were thirsty.
- God traveled with them, protecting them with a cloud in the daytime and leading them by a pillar of fire at night.[6]

Both men had remained faithful and faith-filled, but God said that Caleb, in particular, had a different spirit. When they initially arrived at the borders of the Promised Land, Caleb was forty years old. And when he returned with the group Moses had sent to spy out the land, he gave a *wholehearted* report: "We should go up and take possession of the land, *for we can certainly do it*" (Numbers 13:30, emphasis added). He knew they were well able to take the land because God had already given it to them. His trust and confidence was in God's power and might, not his own.

However, everyone else who returned from the scouting mission was negative and fearful. They described the inhabitants they saw there as giants and said, "We seemed like grasshoppers in our own eyes, and we looked the same to them" (Numbers 13:33). Caleb saw the same inhabitants but drew a very different conclusion: "We can certainly do it." That's when God made him a promise: "Because my servant Caleb *has a different spirit and follows me wholeheartedly*, I will bring him into the land he went to, and his descendants will inherit it" (Numbers 14:24, emphasis added).

God rewarded Caleb, and Caleb never let go of what God promised. At age eighty-five he was just as determined to settle for nothing less than what God had promised. The others gave in to fear and stopped short; Caleb persevered in wholehearted commitment and kept going. He refused to quit until he got from *here* to *there*. Listen in as he proclaims his triumph:

> "I was forty years old when Moses the servant of the LORD sent me from Kadesh Barnea to explore the land. And I brought him back a report according to my convictions, but my fellow Israelites who went up with me made the hearts of the people melt in fear. I, however, followed the LORD my God *wholeheartedly*. So on that day Moses swore to me, *'The land on which your feet have walked will*

be your inheritance and that of your children forever, because
you have followed the LORD *my God wholeheartedly.'*

"Now then, just as the LORD promised, *he has kept*
me alive for forty-five years since the time he said this to
Moses, while Israel moved about in the wilderness. So
here I am today, eighty-five years old! *I am still as strong*
today as the day Moses sent me out; I'm just as vigorous to go
out to battle now as I was then. Now give me this hill country that the LORD promised me that day. You yourself
heard then that the Anakites were there and their cities
were large and fortified, but, the LORD helping me, I will
drive them out just as he said."

Then Joshua blessed Caleb son of Jephunneh and
gave him Hebron as his inheritance. So Hebron has
belonged to Caleb son of Jephunneh the Kenizzite ever
since, because he followed the LORD, the God of Israel,
wholeheartedly.

JOSHUA 14:7–14, emphasis added

God had promised Caleb the land of Hebron, and he wasn't
slowing down, losing heart, or giving up until he acquired it—
no matter how big the setbacks were or how long they lasted.
He survived forty years of wilderness. Forty years of people
grumbling and complaining. Forty years. And it was supposed
to be an eleven-day journey from bondage to freedom.

Here's another thing to consider. He survived forty years of
circling Mount Sinai with the most negative people. And not
just negative in perspective. There were about three million of
them, and I'm sure they had all the same problems we'd find
in a city of three million people today. They were families—
communities—filled with the same tragic stories you find in

your neighborhood. The kind of stories that can make people grow old in their hearts long before they are old in their bodies.

A child in trouble.

An unfaithful spouse.

An unexpected pregnancy.

A broken friendship.

A financial loss.

A disappointment.

A betrayal.

A heartache.

An illness.

A death.

When we find ourselves wandering in the wilderness, these are the kind of heartaches that have the potential to make us feeble of heart. That's when we grow bitter, cynical, disillusioned. Life didn't happen like we expected and now a battered heart defines our destiny. We let go of the vision that once fueled our passion. We allow purpose to slip out of our grasp. And we grow old in ways we were never meant to grow old.

Old in our thinking.

Old in what we say and how we say it.

Old in our patterns of behavior.

This can happen just as easily to a twenty-year-old as it can to a senior adult. When we give up on God's promises and give in to disillusionment, cynicism, bitterness, and complaint, we can lose heart at any age.

Kylie initially lost heart, but she knew she couldn't stay in that hopeless place. She was tempted to step out of her marriage that first year—but she didn't. She was disillusioned, but she kept crying out to God, even when she couldn't hear his voice in response. She could have grown old of heart—but she kept moving *through*. Like all of us, she wanted to be delivered from her emotional difficulties, but God wanted to grow her *through* them. So, she strengthened her heart. She did what was in her hand. She kept pressing in to live wholehearted.

Just like Caleb.

Caleb stayed on mission, regardless of all the setbacks. He stayed flexible, robust, passionate, and enthusiastic. And ultimately, it was his wholeness of heart that got him to the Promised Land. Even after forty years of disappointments and living among three million bitter complainers, he knew the secret was keeping his heart healthy—and going *through*.

Through the pain.

Through the struggles.

Through the doubt.

Through the fear.

Through the loss.

Through the betrayal.

Through the forgiveness.

Through the confusion.

Through the insecurity.

Through the disappointment.

Through the disillusionment.

Through all the emotions.

Through rediscovering the wonder—over and over again.

Caleb may or may not have been the most gifted, the most eloquent, or the smartest among his peers. But he was certainly the most wholehearted. I love his bold declaration, "I am still as strong today as the day Moses sent me out; *I'm just as vigorous to go out to battle now as I was then*" (Joshua 14:10, emphasis added).

What confidence! Caleb was eighty-five and "just as vigorous." He kept his zeal and his joy. He hung onto the promise:

"Just as the LORD promised, he has kept me alive" (Joshua 14:10). And he wasn't just alive, he was all in. If he were alive today facing the kind of challenges we do, I can imagine him saying something like this:

> *I'm still here! I'm just saying. . . . They tried to take me out, but I'm still alive. Along the way, I've lost a lot of people whom I loved. I've seen a lot of dreams die. I've seen so many relational disasters. I've felt so many disappointments. I've struggled to make ends meet more than once. I've walked through many health challenges. I've felt lonely and sometimes despised. I didn't get the opportunities I hoped for.*
>
> *But. I. Am. Still. Here. And my heart is whole and full of faith.*
>
> *Satan, on your best day, you didn't take me out on my worst day. I am still here, holding onto the God who fulfills every promise. I'm still trusting. I'm still full of hope.*

Sometimes, I think God uses the people who simply outlast the devil. Like Caleb, they are wholehearted and full of defiant hope. They want to be used by God and make a difference. They stay in the Word, and the Word keeps them alive. They remain full of purpose—decade after decade. They don't give up on possessing their Promised Land—ever. They have a different spirit—a spirit of fully alive.

I often say that the reason God is using me like he is today is simply because I'm still here. Because I have allowed God to heal me and to continue healing me. When you get to be my age, it seems as though many have dropped out of the race and God has fewer options to choose from. But I can tell you from personal experience that if you stay in the race, if you keep your heart whole, God can and will use you. He will get his glory through whoever is willing, available, and tenaciously wholehearted.

THE WILDERNESS TRANSFORMS

Wherever you are on your journey, God still has more assignments for you. "'For I know the plans I have for you,' declares the LORD, 'plans to prosper you and not to harm you, plans to give you hope and a future'" (Jeremiah 29:11).

This verse isn't just for high school graduation cards.

"I know the *plans*." God has lots of plans. Plans for a hope and a future. For every day of your life. Right up to the last breath you take.

Your life isn't over—if you're willing to be "all in."

When you come to Christ, you become a Christian— and the life of a Christian is meant to be a lifelong, continual expansion—not contraction—of the heart. Our hearts are made to grow bigger and stronger, but if we don't manage our disappointments well, our hearts begin to shrink. Then it isn't long until we start to grow fearful, to lose sight of our assignments and destiny, to feel weary of life and faith.

We can't control what life sends us, but we can control how we respond. After all, the only way through is . . . *through*.

If Caleb had known an eleven-day journey was going to be forty years of circling the same mountain, he might not have signed up. But when the unexpected interruptions began, he adapted. Despite the detours, he held onto the promises—and kept his heart growing and whole. He stayed all in.

Kylie did too—once she learned what she could only learn through her wilderness experience.

"The most important lesson I learned was to value people," she said. "I truly learned to love the people there—to cherish what made them happy and to admire them. They worked hard to provide for their families, and they got pleasure out of so many things I'd overlooked in life. My time there wasn't about who I was or what I could offer. It was about learning to love and accept people for who they are—just as Christ loves and accepts us.

"Then when we'd been there twelve years and things were stable and good, I was hit with another unexpected. I was thirty-six weeks pregnant with our fourth child when Sam told me he believed the Lord wanted him to resign and look for work back in the city we'd come from."

"I immediately said, 'No! You're not resigning. I can't leave my job, either. I'm pregnant. Who's going to hire me this close to having a baby?' It was hard to believe *I* was the one saying all this. But I was truly happy where I was. God had changed me. Now that I was comfortable and settled again, the thought of leaving was too scary. *Me*. Of all people! The woman who fought for eight long years to escape my wilderness and all God wanted to do in me!" Kylie laughed. "Now, I didn't want to leave, even if the Promised Land might be the next stop!

"I was so stressed, but Sam followed what God was calling him to, and it opened doors to a future I could not have imagined.

"We moved back to the city and Sam took a position at a large church. I was thrilled to be back with my family and old friends, but I had come back a different person. The wilderness changes you—for the better—if you let God do the work in you."

Kylie learned how to live wholehearted in an unexpected place.

"I would have never been prepared for the next step in my journey if we hadn't moved away all those years ago. It was during that time I learned how to find God when I couldn't see where my wilderness was leading, and how to take steps forward even when I could not hear his voice.

"I remembered biblical principles I'd been taught when I was growing up, and I decided to do what they said. I prayed. I read my Bible. I wrote in my journal. I gave God what was in my hand—and he helped me develop a great health-and-fitness-training business. I trusted him even when I didn't have any emotional assurance that he was there. I learned how to truly practice *faith*, which the Bible defines as 'confidence in what we hope for and assurance about what we do not see.'[7] I learned to walk by faith and not by sight during those years. I had to let God work in my heart before I could live in peace and really flourish."

What Kylie and I both have learned over the years is how to keep our peace—especially over the things we can't control. I'm determined to keep my peace at all costs, because if the enemy can get my peace, he can get my heart. I've learned that just because everything in my life is going crazy doesn't mean I have to. I can't tell you how many times I've said to myself, *Christine, just because everyone else is having a meltdown doesn't mean you have to. You have my permission to not freak out.* Remember how I said God never sleeps or slumbers, so there's no point in both of us staying up all night? So let's cast our cares and anxieties on him and go to bed.[8] Worry and stress will age us. Peace that surpasses all understanding will keep us wholehearted.

The unexpected is never going to stop happening, so let's be disciplined enough in the wilderness to strengthen our hearts and live wholehearted no matter what is going on around us: *Lord, even if I cannot see you, I trust you. Even if I can't hear you, I trust you.*

Kylie's Promised Land—the place God had been preparing for her, and preparing her for—was far more than she would have experienced had she never moved to a small town where she learned to truly value people. Eighteen years after she and Sam married and first moved away from all she'd known, Kylie joined the pastoral team of the church in which she'd been raised. And for the next decade, she served faithfully, loving people in the way God had transformed her heart to do.

"When I was in my twenties, I would just dream," Kylie said. "I'd dream of all I was going to do for the kingdom. And when I married, I let those dreams die. I let them go. But eventually, I let God deal with me so he could resurrect them. I've been living these dreams for a decade now, and I'm still living them. I can teach. I can disciple. I can create. I can connect women to each other. I can motivate them. I can do what's in my hand to do, but I have to keep my hand open to God. Now I say to God, *Whatever you have next, I'm in—all in.* I finally got to that place of genuine trust.

"Every now and then Sam and I will drive out to the countryside and visit our old town," Kylie said. "When we drive past the church and our old house, I feel a nostalgic tug at my heart. I can see the hand of God all over those twelve years, and I'm so thankful for the process I walked through. I worked hard in that season of my life—at raising our children, having a strong marriage, developing my business, and letting God transform me so my interior was as fit and healthy as my exterior. I worked hard at what was in my hands, and I let God take me from brokenhearted and halfhearted to wholehearted."

Kylie's journey shows us that in every season of change there is an opportunity to adjust to the unexpected. There is an opportunity to let go of more of our control and embrace more of God. To trust him more than we ever have before. It's easy to get caught up in where we're going, believing in the trajectory we may have planned for our lives. But it's so important to trust him—even when we honestly don't want to. That strengthens our hearts and keeps us in a place of living wholehearted. It keeps us in a place of living expectant within our unexpected. Of anticipating all the good God has for us in every experience. Of being willing to risk something new. Of living with a faith-filled perspective, fully trusting God—no matter what.

Chapter Seven

WHEN THE UNEXPECTED REQUIRES RISK

Stretching Beyond

It's strange how new and unexpected conditions
bring out unguessed ability to meet them.
—EDGAR RICE BURROUGHS

I just want to make a difference."

It was a familiar heart cry I had read many times before in hundreds of volunteer applications from young people wanting to serve at A21—typically college-age singles who wanted to assist with operational support, graphic arts, photography, filming, social media, or technology. But never had I read these words on an application from a *grandmother*.

I couldn't help but be intrigued, and I couldn't stop reading her story.

"I know God has work for me to do," she wrote. "Every time I open my Bible, he shows me through verse after verse that there's more. I want my life to count."

Her name was Laura, and she lived in Southern California. She had been married for more than thirty years, raised two daughters and a son, and welcomed three grandchildren into this world. I'm sure her life had already counted in very meaningful ways, but she wanted to do more.

"I know everyone expects me to start living at a slower pace now that my husband and I are empty nesters. I'm supposed to have lunch with girlfriends and fill my days hanging out with my grandchildren, but everything inside of me says, *No, that's not what God has for me.* I feel very vulnerable thinking this way, but I know God wants me to step out toward something I've never known."

Someone over the age of fifty with a vision to *still* make a difference? Someone who has raised a family, led a successful life, and still thinks there's more to do to make her life count? That spoke to me.

As I continued reading through the stack of volunteer applications, I was impressed by all of them—sent in from around the world—but I couldn't help going back to Laura's. I wanted to read her story again.

"Four years ago, my youngest daughter was diagnosed with an auto-immune disease that left her virtually bedridden for a year. Then my older daughter suffered two miscarriages, and we learned that she also suffered from the same auto-immune disease. In researching solutions, I discovered that I, too, had suffered from this same disease all my life, only in a milder form. All my adult life, I have dealt with bouts of fatigue, brain fog, and days that felt like every step was completely uphill. Together, we followed our doctor's directives, researched natural solutions, and completely changed our lifestyle and diet. Today, all three of us are healed. I feel God has given me a new lease on life, and I want to serve him with this gift of health he's given me. I've never felt better in my entire life."

I certainly understood what it was like to face an unexpected diagnosis and then to feel a renewed sense of purpose.

"I've taken an inventory of my life and I want to be used by God differently than ever before."

Such tenacity and passion. Such intentionality.

As I kept reading, I learned that Laura had volunteered in various capacities throughout the earlier decades of her life—fundraising for her children's Christian school, leading Bible studies, and supporting outreaches in her community. She obviously had served the Lord faithfully for a long time.

"I feel a sense of responsibility to step way out of my comfort zone. I know there's more that God has called me to do."

I have always prayed for our team—for God to send us exactly who we needed and who needed us—and he has always sent us truly gifted people. People who wanted to do *more*. People determined to fulfill their purpose and potential. People willing to give their time and talents to help expand God's kingdom. People like Laura.

"I learned about A21 when I attended a Propel event," she wrote. "As Christine described their work to help abolish slavery around the globe, my heart started racing, and I knew God was showing me something about my future. I believe I'm supposed to continue serving God by volunteering for A21."

Yes! Laura understood the charge I believe we are all to accept—to keep living our lives on mission and running hard after Jesus no matter what our age. To fulfill all God has created us to be and all that he has called us to do here on earth—and to take everyone we can with us to heaven. She had my attention and my heart—and I wanted her in our office as fast as possible.

I also couldn't wait to find out how the dynamics of an office staffed by dozens of passionate millennials would change when a grandmother joined the team!

OUR GOLDEN VOLUNTEER

To say that Laura felt intimidated her first day, her first week, or first month is an understatement. She knew how to make phone calls, input data, and organize files, but not how to run the world with a few apps like the other volunteers did.

She felt ill equipped, but she still believed she could make a difference.

She felt inadequate, but she was still willing to take a risk.

She felt uncomfortable, but she was still willing to be led by people half her age.

She felt afraid that she would fall on her face, but she still stepped out in faith. Faith gave her the courage to be inconvenienced and interrupted. To risk humiliation. To risk rejection. To just show up.

Laura knew God had work for her to do, so she showed up every day to do his work—and the team loved her. They taught her technology, and she taught them how to pause their technology and connect—with each other and with God. The team needed her wisdom, and she needed their youthful zeal and enthusiasm for life.

As Laura worked and learned, she discovered that she had more capacity than she realized. She was amazed at how fast she could change gears—and skills she once considered beyond her reach quickly became a part of her routine. All because she took an unexpected risk.

God showed Laura what he wants all of us to know at every age, in every season and stage of life—there is always *more*. As long as we are alive, we have a purpose to fulfill. We have a mission to complete. We have God-assignments to pursue. As soon as we finish one, God will have another. The challenge is that there is often a temptation to settle for less, or to allow social norms and others' expectations to dictate what occupies our time and attention in each season of life— from starting a career, getting married, and having children to eventually retiring. But those norms and expectations can be wrong. It is God alone who orders our steps and gives purpose to each season of our lives.[1]

As I watched Laura navigate her new role, I was encouraged by the way she was young in spirit but mature enough to shepherd all the younger volunteers with the kind of wisdom that only comes with age. The twentysomethings were miles away from home and needed someone like her—a spiritual parent. She mentored them, encouraged them, and often prayed with them. I have always valued the contributions of different generations, knowing we need the wisdom of the older generation, the resources of the middle generation, and the energy of the younger generation *all working together*—and I loved seeing it happen in our office.

One night at a team dinner, Laura told me more of her story, and I began to realize the cultural norms she had defied when she sent us her application. In the months prior to applying for our volunteer position, there were many times when she had lunch or coffee with friends and felt the same kind of peer pressure every kid does—to do what is expected, when it's expected, and how it's expected. I'm so glad she courageously chose to do the unexpected.

"My friends and I had always looked forward to the day when our kids would be grown so we could play tennis and golf, and just enjoy ourselves," Laura said. "But the closer that day came, the more disappointed I felt. It was so surprising to have looked forward to something for years and then to realize it's not how I even wanted to spend my time. One day at lunch, as my friends and I talked about trips we were planning and what we were going to do with our grandkids, I felt like I was talking about someone else's life and not my own. It was clearly not what God wanted me to do. But it was the expected thing to do. That's when I began to question all of it, and I realized retirement wasn't God's will for me. Not now. Not as long as I still have a pulse and am able to do more for the kingdom."

Listening to her, marveling at her courage and strength, I couldn't help but think about Caleb—the wholehearted leader Moses sent to spy out the Promised Land. He never embraced the idea of retirement either. He lived like all his years were the golden years, and at the end of his life, he was still as strong as ever and full of vision for the future. Even at eighty-five, he held onto all that God had promised him when he was forty—when he first laid eyes on Hebron.[2]

KEEP YOUR EYES ON HEBRON

Hebron was a desert region rich with history and natural resources, including an abundant water supply. Great men and women of faith had lived there—and been buried there. Abraham and his wife Sarah, their son Isaac and his wife Rebekah, and Isaac's son Jacob and his wife Leah. It was also where God had made a covenant with Abraham and promised him he would be the father of many nations.[3] Abraham—the man called the friend of God.[4] Understandably then, the word *Hebron* actually means "the binding friendship place."[5] In so many ways, Hebron was sacred ground, blessed land, fertile and significant.

When Moses first sent Caleb and eleven other spies into the Promised Land to scope it out for the children of Israel, Hebron was inhabited by giants—people of great size, sometimes topping nine feet tall,[6] including the sons of Anak. A famous descendant of Anak was the giant Goliath—the Philistine whom David defeated with a slingshot.[7] When the spies returned and gave their report to Moses, ten of them were fearful. "We can't attack those people," they said, "they are stronger than we are" (Numbers 13:31). But Caleb had a different perspective: "We should go up and take possession of the land, for we can certainly do it" (Numbers 13:30).

When everyone else wanted to back off, Caleb wanted to charge right in. But, as I mentioned in the last chapter, it would take another forty-five years before Caleb would receive the land that God had promised. During all those wilderness years, he kept believing. And he kept himself vitally alive— spiritually, physically, mentally, and emotionally—eager to possess what God had promised him. Over the course of four decades, he never let go of the promise that Hebron was his. His attitude was *all in*—he looked to the future with nothing but hope and courage.

Even so, it's not unreasonable to think that at eighty-five, he might well have been ready for retirement. He could have said something like, "I made it through the wilderness, and I've done my time. I've led men in battle and helped families find their piece of the Promised Land. I've set up and torn down more tent cities than any military commander on the earth. I've contributed diligently to my IRA and 401(k). I've watched my children grow up and have children of their own—and I've got plenty of stories to tell. Now is the time to kick back and play golf in the desert, even if it's just one big sand trap."

But he didn't. He wasn't content to just have stories to tell. He wanted to keep living the great story God had written for him. Caleb knew where his help came from,[8] and he had the kind of wisdom that only comes with time. So instead of settling into retirement, he did battle with giants—and prevailed:

> In accordance with the LORD's command to him, Joshua gave to Caleb son of Jephunneh a portion in Judah—Kiriath Arba, that is, Hebron. . . . From Hebron *Caleb drove out the three Anakites—Sheshai, Ahiman and Talmai, the sons of Anak.*
>
> JOSHUA 15:13–14, emphasis added

Isn't it fascinating that Caleb was the one willing and able to take on these three giants—Sheshai, Ahiman, and Talmai—and that he had to wait until he was eighty-five to do it? Could it be that sometimes there are giants we can defeat only because we've been seasoned long enough by our wilderness years to know we can? That we've followed God long enough to be strong and confident—in who we are in Christ and in what we can do in his strength?

When Caleb was old enough, strong enough, and mature enough, he defeated those three giants and took possession of the land—as his reward, and as an inheritance for all the generations to come. He'd lived long enough to be confident that every battle is the Lord's,[9] no matter how big the giants are.

Do you think that maybe you have a Hebron too? Maybe you've raised your family, had a fulfilling career, and diligently grown your nest egg. You're "all set." But what if God has more for you? Especially, now that you are older and wiser. You know things—the kind of things you couldn't have known when you were younger. What if there are some enemies that only you can slay—enemies only a mature, seasoned, passionate believer could ever take down? Enemies that need to be destroyed to prepare the way for the generations to come after you? Now is the time to take your Hebron. Now is the time to do more, not less. Now is the time for your life to wind up—not down—because "the way of life winds upward for the wise" (Proverbs 15:24 NKJV).

Even though I already had run a ministry for years—Equip & Empower—God had more for me to do. More ministries for me to innovate and pioneer. More ways for me to share the gospel. More knowledge for me to learn so I could keep growing.

When I was forty-one, I started A21.

When I was forty-eight, I started Propel.

When I was fifty, I started a global TV program.

When I was fifty-one, I started graduate school.

At this point, my attitude is like Caleb's. *What's next? I'm ready for it. I'm excited for the unexpected. I'm all in. Let's go!* I am fully convinced that nowhere in the Word does it ever say *stop*. Nowhere does it say to *retire*, as we've come to understand retirement. That's why God was prompting Laura's heart to hunger for *more*. That's why he wanted her to come volunteer for us. He didn't want her to slow down or stop. He didn't want to waste all the years he'd been preparing her for all he had prepared for her. He wanted her to keep fulfilling her purpose, to step into the God-assignment that only she could fulfill, because what she brought to the team comes only with age—a reward and powerful gift from God. When she seemed to be perfectly set up for a season of ease, everything on the inside of her said there had to be *more*, so she stretched beyond her comfort zone where everything was safe and familiar.

I understand that kind of stretching. In everything God has called me to do, I've not known exactly where to begin, but each time, God has led me *to stretch*.

I've learned that the unexpected growth God wants for us is in the stretch—not in our pulling back. The grace and the blessing are in the stretch. To do what God has called us to do isn't possible without the stretch. He's calling us to stretch past our fear, past our insecurity, past our convenience. He wants us to stretch so we can move forward.

But we must fight to move forward, to make room for him to do more in and through our lives. We must resist the pressure of others' expectations and the inertia of settling for our comfort zones. Those are the signs of aging in ways we were never meant to age. We have to combat them—especially when we're tempted to think we've done enough.

Just because we've raised our kids, completed our career, and welcomed grandkids into our hearts doesn't mean we are through. At my age, I could rationalize that I've done enough—for the kingdom, for the church, for the global community—but I really haven't. None of us has if we're still alive. If we were done here on earth, God would take us home. He always has more for us to do, even if we don't move as fast as we used to, even if it takes us a little longer to get it done.

YOU WERE MADE FOR MORE THAN BINGO

As I've grown older, I have had to acknowledge some of the same signs of aging that we all do—and fight against them. It's hard work to resist growing old and choosing to live agelessly. To choose being completed over being depleted. To pioneer instead of settle. To advance instead of retreat. To simply keep taking risks. But I willingly push myself to fight the good fight of faith so I can stay young at heart.

For example, I've had to choose to resist the gravitational pull to the security of routines. I remember when my mum was alive, I would call her almost every week—and in each phone call, she lamented that she didn't see me enough. So, when I planned a trip home to Australia, which I did several times a year, she was always so excited I was coming. And I couldn't wait to see her too. But if I wanted to visit on a Wednesday, she would tell me I couldn't come. Even though I'd call weeks in advance to let her know, and even though I'd reminded her over and over as the date approached, and even though I called her as soon as we landed, she was always quick to let me know that Wednesdays were out of the question.

Wednesday night was bingo night, and it didn't matter that I'd flown fourteen hours to see her, bingo night was bingo night, not family night. Nick and I always laughed about it, but it was still hard to understand. You would think she would move heaven and earth to see me, and she would—just not on bingo night!

How many of us have "bingo nights" in our lives—those weekly or monthly events for which we just aren't willing to flex, even if one of the most important people in our lives wants to interrupt our routine? What if Jesus wanted to stop by and introduce a new adventure to us? Would we be willing to skip whatever it is to listen? How can we be truly open to God and his kingdom purposes for us if we're unwilling to let go of bingo night?

We think we're completely open to whatever God asks—because we're good Christians—but when someone wants to interrupt our bingo night, we find out how rigid and resistant we really are. We don't really want to be inconvenienced. We might say we want to go to the morning Bible study at church, but only if we don't have to get up earlier than normal. We might say we want to volunteer at the hospital, the local elementary school, or at the senior center, but not if the only opening is on the same day as bingo. How can we ever create more space for God to move in our lives if we aren't willing to flex all these bingo nights in our lives?

As much as I like my favorite (Greek) foods and favorite (Greek) restaurants, I always push myself to try something new. I love date night with Nick, but I don't want to be so committed to our date night that I miss a date with Jesus. I also don't want to become someone who might refuse to go to Thursday night prayer at church because that's the night of my favorite TV show. Let's risk shaking up our routines to keep ourselves available for God—even on bingo night!

LET'S STAY FLEXIBLE

I like to think I'm flexible—and invincible—and open to new adventures. And most of the time, I am—until I go to the trampoline park with Sophia. More than once I've gone with her to jump and flip and bend like a pretzel only to find out that I'm not a pretzel anymore! And I always pay for it the next day when I can barely stand up straight. This body that bore two children and has traveled the globe for more than twenty years no longer likes to be flung into the air and then bounced off a springing canvas. But each time she asks me to go, I feel compelled to go just so I don't quit trying. I want to keep working on staying flexible, and so I keep stretching—in every way.

I read books all the time to keep myself current with knowledge about leading teams, parenting my kids, and staying strong emotionally. I can't expect to remain an effective leader to my team if I don't keep enlarging in knowledge and the skillful application of it. I can't expect to keep up with a generation that speaks differently and was educated differently from my generation if I don't enlarge my mind to understand them and learn how to communicate effectively with them. As tempting as it is, I cannot rest on the success of my past to take me into the future in any area of my life.

I recently started working on my master's degree in evangelism and leadership at Wheaton College. I enrolled in a Propel Cohort with more than twenty other women from our Propel chapters. When I started, it had been thirty years since I last sat in a classroom. Even though I have a degree from Sydney University in Australia and have experience with university-level education, entering the American college system was intimidating. I had no idea what to expect, and the more I thought about it all, the more terrified I became that I wouldn't be able to write a paper—even though I can write books! Fear is never logical. I almost talked myself out of starting the course, but my desire to keep growing is greater than my fear of failure. I want to keep growing in my capacity to speak and lead others to Christ. I want my mind to stay active and my spirit alert. I want to stay flexible. I want to be like Laura.

Ever since Laura joined our A21 team, she's kept learning. She knows it's part of God's growth plan to keep her flexible, alive, and young—and she's willing to let others teach her. "I love how the team helps me when I have a new project I don't know how to begin. They show me shortcuts on the computer or a website that will make me more productive. They are amazing! I laugh sometimes at how some things are so over my head. But God equips me, and he uses my teammates. I love what I have stepped into."

What Laura stepped into was remaining flexible so she could keep flourishing—not just for herself but also for the next generation.

When I read Laura's volunteer application, one of the most powerful statements she made—the one that moved me so deeply—was her desire to leave her grandkids more than just memories. She wanted to leave them a *legacy*—even though at the time of applying to A21, she didn't know what that was. It was just a desire that God planted in her heart, and she was obedient to pursue it even though she couldn't define it. She was willing to follow the leading of the Lord even before she had understanding—and God gave her the desire of her heart.

"My grandchildren love to hear about all of the 'world changers,' as I call them, in the local office where I work, and those serving around the world," Laura said. "It has brought a rich dynamic to our relationships that I could have never anticipated. One of my granddaughters even told me that she really likes how happy I am now that I work with 'world changers,' and that she is going to be a 'world changer' someday too. Because I was willing to grow, God has given her a vision for a future that is so much bigger than before. I absolutely love it that my granddaughter wants to follow in my footsteps doing kingdom work!"

Having her granddaughter want to follow in her footsteps is definitely inspiring a legacy. Laura's renewed vision for her future—even when it was fuzzy and unclear what that future actually was—is what moved her forward. As she willingly pursued that vision, it came into focus and led her to A21. Getting to leave a legacy was the unexpected blessing on the other side of her obedience.

What spark has God put in your heart? Where does he want you to work, serve, or volunteer? Who does he want you to reach, love, encourage, and mentor? Who is on the other side of your obedience? Where might you need to be flexible and stretch yourself to take the next step?

I believe you are the answer to someone's prayers. You are an unexpected blessing in someone's life. God wants to use you, and he wants you to have vision for every age and stage of life—including this one.

EXERCISE A NEW MUSCLE

Now that I'm over fifty, I go to the doctor more often for checkups. Who knew there were so many things to examine? They want to monitor my heart, my bone density, and my hormones. If I ask about any kind of new issue, they usually just say it's a sign of age. On one particular visit, I explained to my doctor how I wanted to be sure I was still fit, because, after all, I have a preteen and a teenager to keep up with. So the doctor added a test to analyze my muscle mass. When the results revealed that I had 31 percent body fat, I was shocked.

The healthy range for a fit woman my age was 21–25 percent. *My results couldn't be right!*

So, I went to the gym for a second opinion. (Yes, I was in denial!) When they tested me, they were just as quick as the doctor to inform me that I was "skinny fat." That meant I looked healthy on the outside, but inside my muscles were atrophying. I literally was losing muscle mass. I wasn't overweight, but I wasn't fit either. It was part of growing older, they said. I knew then they were in a conspiracy with my doctor. If I wanted to be fit and resist the aging process, I needed to lift weights. In other words, *If you don't use it, you lose it.* There is no stasis mode when it comes to muscle mass. If you aren't getting stronger, then actually you are getting weaker. If you aren't increasing, then you're decreasing.

I knew it was time to move past denial and propel forward, but I had no idea where to begin. I had always loved to run and bike, but I had never lifted weights and worked out in a gym. On my first visit, I just stared at all those weights, because it was overwhelming. I had no idea how to pick one up properly and not hurt myself. I had no idea how much weight was safe for me to lift. It was all so intimidating, but I had made the commitment to fight the signs of aging, and, with the help of a trainer, I started building strength.

In the beginning, I could only lift a few pounds, and I certainly couldn't do any push-ups. But I stayed with it—for weeks and months—and now it's been a few years. I am so much stronger, and I can now do more push-ups than Nick! I tell my girls that I want to be a super granny for Jesus! Because I keep lifting heavier and heavier weights, I've built muscles I didn't even know I had, but they are muscles that have been there all along.

Once again, isn't that what Laura did? She had mental, spiritual, and emotional muscles God wanted her to keep using. He didn't want the strength he'd developed in her to atrophy in a season of life we call retirement. He didn't mind if she changed the rhythm of her life—especially after decades of devotion to her family, community, and business—but he didn't want her to stop.

YOUR BEST YEARS ARE AHEAD OF YOU

When I look around the office at all our younger volunteers, I think of all we could have missed if Laura had decided to retire instead of re-fire. We would have missed such unexpected blessings of her shepherding, mentoring, and leading—and she would have missed out on so many blessings too.

I want to activate more women like Laura—women like you. Right now, there are more than 76 million baby boomers in the United States and more than 83 million millennials.[10] And we all need each other. The millennials need the boomers to help them mature, and the boomers need the millennials to help them stay young at heart. It's time for all of us to step into our places—and not subject ourselves to the world's system of retirement—so we keep building the kingdom of God and live with an eternal perspective, never fearing the future.

That's what Laura did, and today, she is no longer a volunteer. Laura is on our staff team as the Global Volunteer Coordinator. What she brought to our California office volunteers, she now gives to all our volunteers wherever they are serving A21 around the world. Her contribution and leadership are a huge blessing and answer to prayer. She has never stopped being grateful for all God has done to give her a new lease on life—and neither have we.

"When my daughters and I were sick, it felt like my best years were over," Laura said. "I'm so thankful God healed me and showed me how big he really can be. That I am a vessel for his purposes—that's my mission. I'm so glad he showed me that my best years are ahead of me."

And so are yours if you'll stretch beyond where you are. If you'll break out of your bingo night. If you'll work all the muscles God gave you. If you'll take the risk to obey and start something new.

Chapter Eight

WHEN THE UNEXPECTED IS INCREMENTAL

Taking the Next Step

A keen sense of humor helps us overlook the unbecoming,
understand the unconventional, tolerate the unpleasant,
overcome the unexpected, and outlast the unbearable.
—BILLY GRAHAM

It wasn't the most glamorous night of my life as a traveling evangelist. I was sleeping on a cot, doing my best not to wake the three small children under age five with whom I was sharing a room. I had been trying to sleep face down and breathe into my pillow so I wouldn't catch the flu that one of the kids was fighting, but I was so uncomfortable. Exhausted from not really being able to sleep—mostly due to fighting slow suffocation—I had to turn over and pray for germ-free air. But trying to do so quietly on a creaky camping cot required more dexterity and balance than I had anticipated.

On my first try, I had simply started to roll over, but the cot and all the covers weighing me down wanted to roll over with me. It took all my strength to overcome the centrifugal force that would have landed me on the floor with the cot on top of me.

My next attempt involved gently sliding the covers onto the floor—a mere six inches below me—and trying my first move again. Not exactly brilliant, but in my fatigued state, it seemed worth a shot. But the removal of the covers made no difference. I still seemed destined to land on the floor with a loud crash.

Collapsing on my stomach in defeat, I was tempted to laugh, but instead, I started to cry. None of this is what I had expected.

But it was exactly what I had wanted.

From the time I was twenty-one, I felt desperate to serve God, and I had prayed fervently for him to use me. So, when leaders at my church asked for volunteers to serve on a cleanup team in the youth ministry, I said *yes.* When the assistant youth pastor asked me to help start the Hills District Youth Service, a local, nonprofit, community youth center for at-risk teens, I said *yes.* Then, when my senior pastor called me and said, "Christine, I want you to be the state director of our denomination's youth movement, Youth Alive," I said *yes.* I was passionate about Jesus and willing to serve in any way that would be useful for the kingdom of God to advance on the earth. I had prayed, *Here I am Lord, send me,* and then left the where and to whom up to him.

So, for the previous seven years, I had crisscrossed Australia, mostly traveling alone in my car down country roads in New South Wales, making my way from Sydney to a different country town each week. Sometimes I had driven eight to nine hours at a stretch to develop youth leaders, help build youth ministries, and speak at evangelistic rallies. Seeing teens come to Jesus was what I loved. Being used by God was what I wanted. I never lost my wonder at seeing God save young people.

For those seven years, I had walked out my *yes* and faithfully served God, stepping through every open door in each new town—even when that meant couch surfing in the homes of people who attended local churches and sponsored Youth Alive.

Tonight, my hosts were a gracious couple eager to impact the youth in their community. I was grateful for their accommodation, but being twenty-nine and stuck face down on a camping cot was *not* where I had expected my itinerant evangelist life to lead me. Granted, I'm not sure I really knew what to expect, but this wasn't it. I just never imagined sharing a room with three sleeping kids, stuck face down, trying not to breathe flu germs.

Determined not to let this be the pinnacle of my ministry life, I decided to give it one last effort to roll over and *not* fall on the floor. Somehow, rolling over had become a critical goal to accomplish. So, after doing a careful mental calculation of the necessary strategic moves, I lifted myself up with my arms and flipped myself over as fast as I could spin. The cot bounced and banged noisily on the floor, but I nailed it—and the kids didn't wake up. Success!

Despite my triumphant rollover, my feelings of victory were short-lived. Staring into the dark, I couldn't deny the unexpected loneliness that had begun to creep into my heart. I couldn't deny the doubts that made me wonder if I had made a wrong decision, if I was in the wrong place and not really making a difference. I couldn't deny the real reasons I couldn't sleep.

As the tears slipped off my face and onto the pillow, my doubts piled up, one on top of the other. I could hear my mum's voice in my head: *Christina, you're wasting your life. How can you live like this? How will you ever get married? You're eating rice and beans. You resigned a corporate job and salary package with incredible benefits for this? Besides all that, a girl has no business driving hours and hours on desolate roads all alone.*

I reached for the covers I'd tossed on the floor and pulled them close. Thinking of all my friends who had graduated from Bible school with me, I imagined them thriving as youth pastors, associate pastors, and worship leaders—positions I perceived were better, more stable, and included the benefits of being surrounded by a team. When I had last spoken with one of them, even she had admitted several of them didn't understand why I had accepted this position, that driving around the countryside didn't make any sense.

I thought of all my friends who I'd left behind in the corporate world and how they were living their dreams, climbing the ladder to success. I was happy for all of them, really, but tonight, it was hard not to believe they all had it so much better than me, that they weren't as lonely as me—and I was absolutely certain they were sound asleep in nice, comfy beds. Probably even sleeping in the same cushy bed every night.

My thoughts surprised me. I had digressed from being lonely to questioning my decisions to thinking about my friends sleeping in real beds. I couldn't help but laugh at myself. My predicament *was* funny—and miserably uncomfortable—and my thoughts were so absurd.

Taking a big sigh and drying my damp face with the sheet, I knew better than to give in to all my irrational thinking. I'm sure my friends were going through their own trying experiences. Everyone has his or her story. I had to believe God was going to use all of this—I just wasn't sure what for.

And deep down, I knew even my mum meant well. Her questions were valid—logical motherly concerns—but I *knew* this was right. I *knew* that the desire God had put in my heart, the trust my leaders had placed in me, and the lives I was seeing changed week after week were right. I just needed some sleep. That's all. A good night's sleep.

LORD, SEND ME

The night I wrestled with the cot and my ridiculous thoughts was more than twenty years ago. Looking back, that whole night seems so silly, and yet, it was powerfully significant. Back then, I was an anomaly—a single, traveling, female evangelist—and at times, I felt so alone. There was no one who could have prepared me for what that would feel like—to spend hours on the road alone, to be the only woman I knew doing what I was doing, and to constantly feel the pressure to inspire vision in others, often wondering myself if we really could change the world. Going from town to town to meet with business people, government officials, and church leaders was a pioneering effort, and no one had mentored me in what the pain of spearheading a new endeavor felt like. No one had told me what a lonely road it can be for individuals who are building something new, reaching for a goal, or pursuing a dream—or simply doing something they believed God has called them to do. Yes, I had immense support from my home church and great friends in ministry, but in the day-to-day execution of my role, traveling from town to town, I was isolated.

What I didn't understand then was that God was orchestrating *my* journey for *my* future. He knew what was ahead years down the road—that I would initiate and build ministries and organizations using the very skills I was learning—but I didn't. He knew all my future assignments, and he was preparing me. He was focused on the big picture of that season in my life, while I was focused on one miserable night wrestling with my doubts and unexpected realities.

Now that I'm decades beyond that comical night, I see that moment as a symbol of a place that's familiar to all of us. Whether we're an aspiring professional paying our dues while hoping for a promotion, a student toughing out a boring job to get through school, or a stay-at-home mom who has put her career on hold to change diapers and chase toddlers, we all have rough nights when we can't sleep, and we doubt our decisions—especially when:

- Nothing turns out like we expected.
- We feel all alone in our efforts.
- Our colleagues or friends seem to pass us by.
- We fail at something along the way.

But God is always using our present to prepare us for our future. That night, as I laughed at myself and tried to get my thoughts realigned with God's thoughts, I began to see my circumstances through his perspective. Deep down, I knew God was good and that he does good. I knew he loved me and that choosing to trust him was the best choice. I knew he had a plan and a purpose for my life, and that somehow, all of this—this unexpected season of my life—was part of the preparation. I knew he hadn't forgotten me, even though that night it felt like he had.

By faith, I had pushed myself to keep putting one foot in front of the other. And as much as I didn't want to admit it then, the whole concept of walking by faith and not by sight had sounded far more glamorous when I first said *yes*. Now that it was my day-to-day reality, it felt a lot more grunge than glam. But even though it wasn't easy, I believed God was working out all things for my good, and that somehow he was going to use all of this. So, once again, I joined with the prophet Isaiah, saying, "Here I am, Lord, send me,"[1] and I resolved to keep moving forward.

LITTLE BY LITTLE

What I was learning was something God wants all of us to remember through every leg of our journey: The only way to obtain the promises of God is through faith and patience. That applies to everything, including any words, goals, plans, dreams, or visions he's placed in our hearts. God makes the promises and our part is to persevere, just as the writer of Hebrews told us: "We do not want you to become lazy, but to imitate those who through *faith and patience* inherit what has been promised" (Hebrews 6:12, emphasis added).

Maybe you have a dream, a goal, a plan you've been working toward for years, and you feel God has forgotten you. Maybe you have wanted to:

- Start a business
- Go back to school
- Build a non-governmental organization (NGO)
- Serve in your community
- Become a foster parent
- Go on a mission trip
- Lead a ministry

Whatever it is, God has *not* forgotten you. The dreams, visions, and plans God places in our hearts take time, lots of time. And during all that time, God is working *in us* so he can work *through us*. Again, our part is to exercise faith and patience in the process. *Faith* is believing God, believing that he is who he says he is, and that he will do what he said he would do. *Patience* is our capacity to tolerate delay—to wait. It's trusting that God is good, God does good, and God knows what he is doing—no matter how long it takes and no matter what our purpose may be.

As I have walked this out in my own life—from those years of traveling around the countryside of Australia to stepping into every initiative since—I have found God's process to be strategic and tailor-made for my life. It is the same for your life and God's journey for you. But living our lives with purpose—walking in faith and patience—often feels countercultural to us. We live in a digital world connected globally by the internet and social media, so we have instant access to everything from news to products to real-time videos of world events. As a culture, we consider it normal to get everything we want on demand. Even our reality TV shows give the illusion of overnight success, but there are no overnight success stories really. No one picks up a microphone one day and rises to stardom the next. There are years of hard work in between the beginning of something and whatever it is we deem as success. There are significant life lessons to be learned in the years of working toward a goal. And for us as believers, there are experiences God wants us to go through—that take time—so he can prepare us for the future he's designed for us.

When people ask me how I got to where I am today—leading Equip & Empower Ministries, A21, and Propel—I remember that night on the cot and smile. I don't have five steps to destiny or seven keys to ending global injustice. All I have to share is the process God has walked me through, which is the same one I've seen him walk everyone through when they embraced the dream he placed in their hearts—whether it was becoming a doctor, a teacher, or a journalist, operating a franchise, or staying home to raise a family.

No matter the objective, the process is the same. God places in our hearts a calling, a mission, a goal, an idea, a destiny, and then he leads us to it through small, incremental steps. It's a principle of growth depicted throughout the Bible. The prophet Isaiah said it this way: "He tells us everything over and over—one line at a time, a little here, and a little there!" (Isaiah 28:10 NLT). This same step-by-step process is evident in how God led the children of Israel out of slavery in Egypt and into the Promised Land. They had been enslaved for 430 years, and God knew they had a slave mentality that would hold them back from possessing all God had for them. As much as they wanted to leave Egypt and get quickly to the Promised Land, God didn't race them across the desert. Instead, he led them on an unexpected journey through the desert.

I deeply resonate with this story. Even though God put a desire in my heart to serve him when I first became a believer, I was not ready *then* for all the initiatives I lead *now*. He had to begin healing me by renewing my mind from a slave mentality—from a victim who had been abandoned, adopted, and abused—so I could step into whatever Promised Land he had for me in my future.

Likewise, even though God freed the children of Israel and led them to the Promised Land, he couldn't let them possess all the land immediately. Instead, he worked a very deliberate plan—one that I believe he works in our lives as well. When he marched them across the Jordan River, they faced all the inhabitants living in the land, including the giants Caleb eventually defeated. But God didn't lead them to conquer all the inhabitants in a short period of time—rather, he helped his people to drive them out little by little:

> But I will not drive them out in a single year, because the land would become desolate and the wild animals too numerous for you. *Little by little* I will drive them out before you, until you have increased enough to take possession of the land.
>
> EXODUS 23:29–30, emphasis added

God's directive displayed his infinite wisdom and vision for their future. While they were tired and weary of waiting and wanting to rush right in, God knew they couldn't yet manage all that real estate. He knew that in their current condition, the land they desperately wanted—the land he had promised them—had the power to destroy them. So, he showed them how to achieve their mutual goal little by little. They needed to grow stronger first, so he put them on a strength-training plan. In the process, he prepared the land for them and prepared them for the land.

Can you relate at all to the mindset of the ancient Israelites? Have you ever wanted to rush headlong into whatever it was you felt called by God to do? If so, welcome to the club! Most of us want our destiny on demand. We want all of God's promises to be *yes* and *amen* and *now*. But that's not how God's little-by-little method works. God is process-oriented. Consider just a few other areas of life where we see this principle very clearly. Little by little, we . . .

- Lose weight and build muscle
- Get debt-free by discipline and delayed gratification
- Acquire our education and qualifications
- Build trust in relationships
- Write books

And the list could go on. Virtually everything in our human experience is accomplished little by little. That's how God works—little by little.

When we began A21 in 2008, in Sydney and Thessaloniki, we had one staff member and a handful of volunteers. In the first few months of operation, we had rescued one girl and put one trafficker in jail. We could have grown discouraged and quit before we really gained any traction, but God says not to despise small beginnings.[2] So, we kept going—and we began to succeed little by little. Over the next several years, our rescue numbers increased and we established our aftercare programs. We grew stronger.

As I write, A21 now has thirteen offices and more than two hundred team members in twelve countries. We have rescued hundreds of men, women, and children. We've warned hundreds of thousands of refugees about the dangers of trafficking in the camps in Greece. Our recent Walks for Freedom happened in four hundred cities, fifty countries, and involved tens of thousands of people walking. Our public awareness campaigns warning about trafficking are displayed on buses, in airport terminals, and throughout public venues in multiple countries. We've helped young rescued women finish high school and then sent them on to college—and for the first time in our ten years of rescues, one of these survivors joined our team as a staff member. She wanted to give back by helping other young women step into freedom and healing from the pain they have experienced. But her process—from being rescued to stepping into our offices as a full-time team member—has taken years.

Her journey began when an unexpected opportunity enabled her to escape her traffickers and call the police. The law enforcement officers who rescued her then connected her with A21, and we helped her to begin her long, painful journey of healing. Little by little, she walked through fears rooted in years of being threatened, held hostage, and used in vile ways. Little by little, she reconnected with her family and felt restored to them. Little by little, she learned how to be genuinely loved and how to trust—the hardest step of all. It didn't happen all at once, but it did happen.

All these years later, I have been honored to share the platform with her multiple times as she opens her heart and shares her story with thousands. And every time, my heart is overwhelmed with the goodness of God in her life. All those years ago traveling around the countryside of Australia, I could have never imagined any of this. I wanted to reach people and help them, but I had no idea that this would be what God had in mind. I never dreamed of rescuing victims of human trafficking.

Yes, I've come a long way since that miserable night on the cot, but I got from there to here the same way all God's children do, little by little. And wherever it is God wants me to go next, I'll get there little by little as well.

STEP BY STEP

In God's little-by-little process, steps are essential for success, whether it's in our personal life, professional life, or in our spiritual and emotional development. When I started traveling through those small towns, speaking in high schools, and inviting students to nighttime crusades, I was taking steps. I was building on what I'd learned working with youth at church and in the youth center. Those first two steps prepared me for my work with Youth Alive. And that third step, which lasted seven years, prepared me for the next steps. But it all began with the first step:

- I went to church.
- I said yes to serving at a cleanup day.
- I said yes to volunteering at the Youth Center.
- I said yes to serving as the New South Wales Director of Youth Alive.
- I said yes to being a coordinator in the Hillsong Network.
- I said yes to starting Equip & Empower Ministries.
- I said yes to initiating A21.
- I said yes to launching Propel.

It's not that one thing led directly to the next thing; it's that one *step* led to the next *step*—and I couldn't bypass any of the steps. It was like climbing a set of stairs, and what I learned on each step gave me the wisdom, knowledge, strength, confidence, and maturity to succeed when I moved up to the next one.

Here is an example of just one way that happened. When I worked for the Youth Center in Sydney, before I went to serve with Youth Alive in the countryside, I started meeting with government advisors to discuss youth policies. I went to school after school conducting seminars and working with the faculty to develop after-school programs and to write curriculum. How could I have known then that someday, through the work of A21, we would develop a curriculum called *Bodies Are Not Commodities* that is now distributed throughout schools in the United States, Mexico, Europe, Asia, and Australia? How could I have known that God would use my early years of writing and developing a local curriculum to produce a global one?

God knew the end from the beginning, but I did not.

God knew he was preparing me, but I did not.

God knew all the unexpected moments were leading somewhere. I just trusted him and took steps, and *he has never wasted one step.* "The LORD directs the steps of the godly," writes the psalmist. "He delights in every detail of their lives" (Psalm 37:23 NLT). There are no express elevators to our destination, because God does not take elevators—he directs our steps. And if we're growing, little by little he shows us just one next step at a time.

I know it's not always easy. Trust me, if that night on the cot I had known all that was ahead of me, I might have packed up my bags, driven straight home, and admitted to Mum that she was right about everything—including marriage, makeup, and cooking. But God didn't overwhelm me with too much too soon. Instead, he faithfully held my hand and moved me forward, one step at a time.

Trusting him for the next step has sometimes been deeply painful and difficult. So many times, I wanted to skip steps, but I've seen people do that, and it always leads to a much more painful process. If we skip a step, we will still have to learn what was involved in that step—but chances are we'll have to learn it at a higher cost and in a more public way. Personally, I'd rather learn *everything* I can on each step—every bit of revelation and understanding—so I don't get knocked down by the unexpected events of life ahead. I want the image of Christ to be fully formed in me. I want the fruit of the Spirit fully developed in me. I want to walk in mature love, because that is what I want to flow out of me to a lost and broken world. We simply cannot despise small beginnings—or small steps.

Steps keep us dependent on God. They keep us on our knees in prayer, walking by faith and not by sight.[3] It's human nature to want to know the whole story first—to see the whole staircase from bottom to top—but we can't possibly know the end from the beginning. I certainly didn't.

Today, I fight for justice. My work routinely requires interacting with civic leaders, government officials, and law enforcement officers—all outside the church. It's work I first began to be prepared for all those years ago when I worked at a nonprofit youth center and learned to write government grants petitioning resources for our programs. As I sat in official meetings and submitted proposals, I was being trained to understand the inner workings of government. God was teaching me then how to work within government systems and how to interact with government officials. He was preparing me for the work of A21, but I didn't know it.

Today, A21 routinely sits at the table with top government agencies and other NGOs from around the world. And its effectiveness can all be traced back to the lessons I began to learn in 1989, when I had no idea what I was doing or why. Only God knew then what I would need to know now, and he prepared me throughout the years of my youth work in Sydney, and in all those little country towns. In the process, I have learned over and over that . . .

Steps are necessary—for growth, faith, glory, and strength.

Steps are what grow a good marriage, responsible children, and a fun friendship.

Steps are how we regain our health and grow strong muscles.

Steps are how we get from here to there—wherever there may be.

THE LONG WAY AROUND

Nick is the navigator when we travel. He often uses GPS on his phone to figure out in advance exactly where we need to go once we land at an airport. I always feel so relaxed when he relies on GPS. It shows all these little red lines where the traffic is heavy and suggests alternate routes to get around the backups. It can even direct a person to the nearest coffee shop—something invaluable to my earthly existence.

But sometimes Nick likes to take his own shortcut. Now, these shortcuts aren't always technically "shorter," but he insists they are the way to go. And even though they stress me out quite a bit, I've resigned myself to the fact that there's no talking him out of it. The best thing I can do is congratulate him when they do work, and utter not a word when they don't. After all these years of watching Nick navigate cities around the world—and take many lengthy shortcuts—I've derived some well-thought-out spiritual principles based on our experiences with (and without) GPS. Mostly because I've had a lot of time to think while riding in the car during all those shortcuts.

Like GPS, God knows the traffic jams ahead. He knows the road closures and the accidents blocking the way. So he reroutes us the way he knows is best for us. Instead of letting us take a misguided shortcut, he leads us little by little, step by step, *the long way around.*

When God first led the children of Israel out of Egypt, he knew the route that would best prepare them to live and thrive in the Promised Land—and it wasn't a shortcut:

> When Pharaoh let the people go, God did not lead them on the road through the Philistine country, *though that was shorter.* For God said, "If they face war, they might change their minds and return to Egypt." So God led the people around by the desert road toward the Red Sea.
>
> EXODUS 13:17–18, emphasis added

Rather than leading them on an established trade route—that was hundreds of miles shorter than the one they took around to the Red Sea—God led the children of Israel on the long desert road. He knew the Philistines were an aggressive people, and that if the Israelites were attacked, they might turn back. God knew they still had a slave mentality—not a warrior mentality. For centuries, they had been workers and builders. They had never learned how to fight, so they weren't ready for combat. Before they could conquer and possess the Promised Land, they had to become warriors. God had to renew their minds to think like military generals and soldiers. Until he could do that, he kept them from facing enemies and war. God knew the long way around was for their good—just like it's always for our good too.

When I was on that cot crying and doubting that I was in the right place at the right time, all I could see were my peers who had graduated from Bible college and stepped right onto the teams of so many great churches. I can't imagine how much worse the temptation to play this comparison game would have been if I had social media and spent my evenings keeping up with posts of their seemingly picture-perfect lives. It was already hard enough to not dwell on questions like, *God, why are we taking the long way around? Why did they get a shortcut to all the best jobs? Why don't I get a shortcut?*

The answer was that God had a different future for me, and I wasn't ready for it yet. I wasn't strong enough, and God wanted to build my muscles. So he used the pressures and challenges of my work to mature me—to increase his anointing and power within me. He forged me in the fire. My job was to embrace the process rather than run from it, to keep my feet on the long road.

Friend, the same principle applies to all of us. Even when there is a tempting shortcut, there is never a substitute for the long way around. God uses the desert roads of our lives to protect us and to prepare us. Sometimes our long road takes the form of anonymity, obscurity, long hours, or uncomfortable conditions. It's that place where we think, *Whatever God had for me, I've missed it.* Or, *I feel parched and empty and far from God.* Or, *I've blown it and now God has no use for me.* Or, *I thought God gave me a dream and a promise, but maybe I got it all wrong.* Long roads are also where the waiting can wear us down and dim our hopes. We wait years and pray fervently . . . for the salvation of a loved one, healing in our marriage, breakthrough in our struggles, an open door to our dreams—all to no avail. On the long road, sometimes all we can think is, *God, have you forgotten me?*

God has taken me on many a long road, and I've had all of these discouraging thoughts and more at one time or another. I started walking one long road nearly twenty years ago in South Africa. I saw satellite dishes everywhere, on every rooftop, even in areas of abject poverty, and I realized how many more people I could reach with a message of faith and hope through television. I wanted to create a Christian program right then, but it took almost two decades—the long way around—before I first stepped into a studio to tape my own show, *Equip & Empower.* During those long-road years, God was preparing me so I could use this powerful tool effectively. Who knows, if I had started twenty years ago, I might have run out of material in the first month! But now, I know it is the perfect time for me to use broadcasting to make the name of Jesus known around the world—and I certainly have plenty of messages to share! Was the long road hard and discouraging? Yes and yes. But I'm so glad I never hosted my own program until *now.* God was never withholding it from me—he had placed the desire in my heart in the first place. Rather, he was preparing me. He was renewing my mind, maturing me, and making me stronger, so that when I did step into my dream, I was prepared to handle it well.

God planted the idea of a television show in my mind years before I could step into my own program, and I imagine he has planted ideas and dreams in your mind and heart as well:

- A book you want to write
- An invention you hope to patent
- A house you dream of building
- A business you want to launch
- A family you want to raise
- A difference you want to make

If you have a dream, then chances are you're on a long road. Which means sooner or later, the enemy will mess with you and tempt you to take a shortcut. In those times, you simply must trust that God is protecting you and preparing you, because he is always for you—never against you.[4] And he's not only *for* you, he's gone on *before* you. How do I know? Read this charge that Moses leveled against the Israelites:

> In spite of this, you did not trust in the LORD your God,
> *who went ahead of you on your journey*, in fire by night and
> in a cloud by day, to search out places for you to camp and
> to show you the way you should go.
> DEUTERONOMY 1:32–33, emphasis added

God is *always* out ahead of his people. The problem, with the Israelites and with us, is a lack of trust. Don't repeat the Israelites' mistake. Trust that God is always way ahead of you, protecting you from something you can't see or aren't yet prepared to handle:

- A destructive relationship
- A toxic work environment
- A ruinous business partnership
- A tragedy of epic proportions
- A big responsibility

In every area of my life, the long way around with Jesus as my GPS has always proven better than any shortcut I could have taken without Jesus. I can't tell you how many times Nick's shortcut doubled the distance and the time of our trip. That's not what God wants for our life journeys. Jesus is our tried-and-true GPS, and we don't want to tune him out to gamble on a shortcut.

I'M HERE TO STAY

Wherever you are on your journey, keep going. If you're making gains in incremental small steps, trust God that you're on track. I'm so thankful for the long way around in my life. I'm so thankful for all he saved me from and for all he prepared me to do.

All those years ago, my friends couldn't understand the path I was on. "Christine, what are you doing? Why are you involved in youth center work? Why are you involved in government? Why are you involved in social justice?" It didn't make any sense to my friends—or sometimes even to me—but it made perfect sense to God. He knew my destiny. What they thought was holding me back—my commitment to my local church and its vision for youth—was exactly what prepared me to touch more of the world.

When I was working with kids traumatized and addicted to drugs, kicked out of school, locked up in juvenile centers or prisons, living in foster care, God was preparing me for all the vulnerable people I would someday reach through the work of A21.

When I was speaking in high school gyms, sometimes to only twenty teens, he was preparing me to speak in stadiums filled with tens of thousands of young adults.

When I was orchestrating city-wide crusades in small towns, he was teaching me how to organize and plan large events in public venues. He knew Propel events were in my future.

When I drove long distances working for Youth Alive—an organization that flourishes to this day—he was preparing me for a lifetime of travel around the world. Sleeping on a cot in a room with three kids was just preparation for what was to come. Like when I traveled for three months while suffering from morning sickness. And then learned how to breast-feed in airports, change diapers anywhere I could find a flat surface, and race through terminals with a stroller. Oh, and this. There was the time I was speaking, heard a baby cry in the audience, and my milk came flowing in. That, of course, has nothing to do with traveling, but it was a memorable motherhood experience I'll never forget!

When I first started speaking to women's groups in local churches, God was preparing me for women's conferences globally and for Propel. He was preparing me to grow into a teacher of the Word and of leadership principles based on the Word. That's the assignment that has surprised me the most. I could see from the beginning that I was an evangelist—that I was created to win souls of every age—but I didn't expect to teach the Word and inspire leaders. I didn't expect to activate women to realize their leadership potential. But every unexpected step had a purpose in helping me fulfill my calling, in helping me step into more and more of my destiny.

I don't know what God has placed in your heart to do, but I know he has a journey planned out for you, and he's never forgotten you. Let's determine today to keep taking steps as he faithfully leads us through the expected and unexpected ones alike. Let's trust that he is out ahead of us and that he will use every single one of our steps for our good and for his purposes. Let's anchor ourselves to the promise that he will use every moment of our lives to make us stronger and wiser, more tender and compassionate, more loving and giving—all for his glory. Let's keep embracing the adventure of faith and moving forward—little by little, step by step, even when he leads us the long way around.

Chapter Nine

WHEN THE UNEXPECTED CALLS FOR CHANGE

Letting Go of Limitations

No matter what, expect the unexpected.
And whenever possible be the unexpected.
—LYNDA BARRY

Stepping out onto the porch, coffee in one hand, phone in the other, I thanked God for another beautiful Southern California morning. The sky was a vibrant blue with not a cloud to be seen, and the ever so faint scent of hibiscus hung in the air. Crawling into our hammock, a favorite place where I love to pray and talk with God, I relaxed, taking in a rare moment with no one else at home. Everything felt so quiet and peaceful, both on the patio and inside of me. Everything felt well with my soul.

Nick had taken the girls out for what I felt sure was an errand for tomorrow's Mother's Day celebration. Their mysterious whispers and hushed giggles in the hall were my first clue, but finding both a preteen and teenage girl out of bed and dressed before noon on a Saturday was the real giveaway. Nick,

Catherine, and Sophia each gave me an all-too-purposeful goodbye, one at a time, while giving each other silly grins as they headed out to the garage. I couldn't help but smile as I thought about how funny the three of them could be, especially when they were up to some kind of covert, top-secret, gift-giving mission.

As I lay there absorbing the quiet, it dawned on me that it was already Sunday in Australia, which meant it was already Mother's Day there. I instinctively opened my phone and went to my favorites list. And then in the split second it took to reach her name and almost tap it, I froze.

What was I thinking? Mum wasn't there. She couldn't be. And she would never be there again. It felt as though the bottom fell out of my heart and my stomach at the same time. I felt chilled, then flushed, then overcome . . . and then profoundly empty. What followed next was the most unexpected, uncontrollable raw emotion that I had felt in years. Wave after wave of sheer grief filled my chest, emptying in explosive sobs I couldn't control. As much as I tried to stop it, or even to slow it down, all I could do was curl into a fetal position and convulse with it.

Mum had always been a phone call away, and I had always called her, no matter where I was in the world. When I needed a good laugh. When I just wanted to hear what was going on in our family. When I wanted to update her on Catherine and Sophia and all their latest shenanigans. When it was Easter, Thanksgiving, Christmas, her birthday, or Mother's Day. I always called.

And she called me.

It had been seven months since my brother George had helped her FaceTime with me on my birthday, when her last words to me were, "I love you." Seven months since the night of my fiftieth birthday party when I'd missed multiple calls from my brother Andrew and then one text saying simply, "Mum is gone." Seven months since our family had flown to Sydney, and we all had laid her to rest next to my dad.

Tumbling out of the hammock, partially bent over, I stumbled into the house. As I got a drink of water and washed my face, I hoped to somehow untangle the knot in my stomach and settle my broken heart. But I couldn't. All that I could focus on was how unexpected all of this was. How out of left field all this was. I had grieved at her funeral, when we were all together, so why was it happening again, and so deeply?

My mind went to all the pictures I had brought home from Mum's house—the ones she had promised to parcel out for us but never did. I had retrieved them from her bedroom closet a couple days after her funeral, when my brothers and I, and our families, all met at her house to sort through her things and start preparing her home for sale. I had promised George and Andrew that I would take on the task of grouping all her photos for each of our families as best I could.

Perhaps that would be a way to get a handle on my emotions and accomplish something constructive at the same time . . .

THE UNEXPECTED PHOTO

After finding where Nick had stacked the boxes in the garage, I put a few on the floor and sat down to begin categorizing their contents. There were seventy-eight years of captured memories to sort, and even more that Mum had inherited from our grandparents and great aunts and uncles.

Opening the first box, I took a deep breath, trying to fortify myself against the barrage of grief that most certainly awaited me. As I picked up the first photo, I found myself staring at a picture of my dad. He looked just like I remembered him, always handsome. It was a black-and-white print just like the one Mum had kept in a frame on her nightstand for the last thirty-two years—ever since he had died. I imagined her telling him goodnight in the evenings, talking out all the issues of life with him, telling him about all the grandkids he'd never met, eventually telling him she'd see him soon. What a reunion she and my dad must have had. I had always been proud of how she had found a way to pick up the pieces after he had died, even though I knew she never let go of him in her heart, that he never stopped being the love of her life. I caught myself smiling through tears just thinking of the two of them together again.

Setting my dad's picture aside, I pulled out a handful of black-and-white photos. They were so old, so fragile, I quickly recognized them as ones that had been passed down to Mum from her parents. I set them in a lid and left them untouched for fear they would crumble to pieces.

As I went through box after box, all the images revealed the timeline of our family history.

There were photos of Mum where she grew up in Egypt.

There were pictures of her on a ship headed to Australia. She was only sixteen at the time—a year older than Catherine was now. Her parents had only enough money to put her and her sister and brother on a ship, while they stayed behind. The plan was for my mum to work and save up enough money to send for them, and she did. I couldn't imagine being sixteen and having to leave all your family and friends to get a job in a strange land—to carry the weight of such a responsibility. Mum had been extremely courageous, but getting her to talk about that part of her life was next to impossible. There was so much my family never talked about.

There were photos of my mum and dad's courtship and wedding. My dad loved to tell the story of how he was engaged to another woman when the two of them came to Australia. When they broke up soon after, he was introduced to my mum through a mutual friend. He always said God used the other woman to bring him to Australia so he could meet the love of his life.

There was a box of all our childhood school pictures. What is it with school pictures? Why does everyone always have to look so awkward? Going through them all, trying to put them in chronological order, I wanted to see how all three of us had changed throughout the years. In each of mine, I found myself looking into my own eyes, as though I was searching for something—and I found it. Someone else might never have noticed it, but I could. I could see the little girl who had learned to hide so much. I could see all the pain behind all those crooked smiles.

Then there were so many photos. So many events . . .

When Dad got a new car.

When Andrew lost a tooth.

When George graduated from high school.

Pictures of Mum and me. And lots of cousins. Our family loved any excuse to party, eat, and dance, so birthdays always involved countless cousins and grand festivities.

My favorite decade was the 1970s. Everyone looked hilarious in psychedelic shirts, foot-wide bell-bottoms, and platform shoes. I cannot believe the clothes my mum dressed me in. How many colors can one person wear at one time?

And then there was my permed hair in the '80s. What was that all about? And the taffeta dresses I had to wear at every formal occasion. Greek mothers were obsessed with dressing their daughters in taffeta—green, red, blue, every color in the rainbow. I have an aversion to shiny, itchy, crunchy fabric to this day.

The whole photo sorting experience was strange—so strange—filled with unexpected emotions. One moment, I was laughing hysterically and the next I was crying from the depths of my heart. Minutes filled with gratitude gave way to moments of crippling pain. That's how grief works. That's how unexpected and unpredictable it is.

I wasn't entirely sure my idea of going through the photos was a good one, but now that I had started, I wanted to keep going. Reaching for the next box, I flipped off the lid, and lying on top was a photo I hadn't seen in decades. It was one of Mum—the only one of Mum—pregnant. I had seen it as a child, once I think, but I never knew which of us she was carrying at the time. When I asked Mum about that photo, she moved me along, avoiding any kind of clear answer.

But Mum was always that way—vague, deflective, and uncomfortable—when we asked about our start in life. She never even wanted to go through photos together when I was growing up. And when I grew old enough to be curious and ask questions about being pregnant—like whether she felt sick when she was pregnant, or what it was like to have a baby—she redirected every conversation. I had grown up in a home full of love *and* full of secrets. Everyone in my extended family knew that George and I were adopted. Even the neighbors knew. But George and I didn't know. My parents never mentioned it.

It wasn't until I was thirty-three and George was thirty-five that we learned the truth. It was devastating to both of us, but over time, we came to understand my parents' reasoning, though it was still painful. They felt that by not telling us they were protecting us, loving us, and providing us a safe cocoon to grow up in. Still, it was hard to think that everyone knew but us. For decades.

When I went home for Mum's funeral, I visited her lifelong neighbor and best friend of forty-five years, Carmel. As we talked and comforted each other, she retold a story that I cherish to this day. She said that my grandmother was the one who had taken the call from the hospital, letting our family know a baby had been born and was up for adoption. As the story goes, my grandmother ran outside shouting to Carmel and my mother, who were enjoying tea in the backyard: "We have a girl! We have a girl!" Hearing that story all over again made me feel so loved.

As I sat there holding that photo—seeing how happy my mum looked—I couldn't help but smile. It was Andrew she was carrying, and I was glad she got to give birth to one of us, especially after accepting that she would never be able to have a child of her own. How wonderful for her to have such an unexpected surprise. I can imagine what a shock it must have been, for both her and my dad.

Scooting myself back against the garage wall, I closed my eyes and focused on just one thing—exhaling. I was utterly drained, yet also glad for all the reminiscing. Deep down, for some reason, I knew I needed to be doing this *now*—and not seven months before when Mum had died. *Timing* is just as important as *doing* when it comes to following God. Even if I didn't see any of this grief coming, working through it was exactly what God had planned for me.

In my mind, I could still see the picture of Mum pregnant with Andrew, and my thoughts drifted into thinking about what my biological mother might have looked like when she had carried me. Somehow, I couldn't imagine her as happy as Mum looked in this photo, especially since she felt the need to give me up. I hadn't thought of her in years, but I found myself wondering if she ever thought of me, if she ever wondered what had become of me. That's when I felt an ache, a deep ache, settle into me.

THE UNEXPECTED GRIEF

For the next two weeks, while trying to put so much of my heart and so many of my thoughts onto the pages of this book, I experienced waves of unexpected grief. It was so acute at times I felt as though my heart might rip in two.

As I kept trying to sort through my feelings and memories, my mind kept returning to that picture of Mum pregnant, and I couldn't help but think of my birth mother. Again and again and again. Somewhere in the midst of it all, it hit me. *Maybe there is more to this than just grieving Mum. Perhaps now that Mum is gone, it's time to dig further into who my birth mother is.*

We never know when God will use an unexpected event to trigger something in us, to extend an invitation to come to him, to deal with something that has remained dormant and untouched in our hearts for years. Deep down, though I had no real understanding yet, I knew I had stumbled onto something, and I asked God to help me. Little did I know he was about to take me on another unexpected journey.

Not long after Mother's Day, we had friends over for dinner. In the course of our conversation, they shared how their adopted son went through a period of questioning and searching, and that a counselor who specialized in family-of-origin issues had helped tremendously. Never had I heard of such a person—a Christian family-of-origin counselor? What did that mean? Our friends explained that the counselor had more than twenty years of experience helping people piece together clues from the past to better understand the present. After the emotional upheavals of the past couple of weeks and feeling consumed by so many thoughts about my birth mother, I was intrigued.

My friends had no idea what I had been going through, but God knew. At many times in my life when I needed information, understanding, and answers, God had led me to someone who could help. He was at it again, and as always, his timing was perfect—the right person at the right time with the right connection to the next step. I knew that God had no intention of exposing a tender place in my heart without wanting to heal it.

Listening to our friends share what a help this counselor had been to their family, and now that Mum was gone, I felt a sense of release to go in search of more details. After all these years, though I knew various facts about my birth mother's life, it seemed that it was time to dig a little further into *who* she was—and perhaps how that had affected who I had become. And after two weeks of being ambushed by episodes of grief, I knew I didn't want the acute pain of heartbreak to become chronic. Hope stirred in me that God was leading me to the right person to pursue this journey with me.

AN UNEXPECTED CONNECTION

When I arrived at my first appointment and the counselor invited me in, I took the seat she offered me close to the windows. I found being there oddly comforting. It's always hard to reveal your private thoughts to a complete stranger, but this woman was skilled at making people feel safe. She was willing to unpack whatever mystery those who came to see her were trying to unravel, and for that I was grateful. I felt sure I was in the right place at the right time. As I began laying out medical records and social work documents I had brought— pieces of my past I hadn't shared with anyone in years—she assured me that we would explore whatever was there to be uncovered.

Over the course of the next few visits, the counselor proved to be the wise and perceptive guide my friends had described— and more. It was clear from her years of experience that she knew how to read between all the lines of information I had given her. She described patterns of behavior for me to contemplate, and during one appointment, she dropped a bombshell of perspective I had never considered: "Christine, do you realize that your biological mother was quite probably exploited by your father, and here you are rescuing women around the world from being exploited as well?

"Your mother was twenty-three, and your father was a fifty-five-year-old successful businessman with a wife and family. He was more than three decades her senior, old enough to be her father. From my years of experience, I guarantee that this wasn't his first indiscretion. The records indicate that she lived in immigrant housing and had only an elementary school education. Do you realize how all that made her extremely vulnerable and at risk?"

As I sat listening to her initial assessment of the documents I had given her, I was stunned. Never would I have theorized that my birth mother was possibly exploited, just as vulnerable as the women A21 reaches out to every day. I had always pictured her as scared, alone, and ashamed when she carried me, but never had I thought of her as a potential victim, as someone similar to the women I'm called to help.

"Whether their relationship was consensual or not," she continued, "whether they met once, twice, or more, your mother most likely was looking for a father figure, affection, protection, or provision. Or, maybe all of them. He was in a position of power and strength. And the fact he wasn't at your birth, and that his name isn't on your birth certificate, shows that she was left to fend for herself."

For the first time in my life, I felt compassion for my birth mother, almost the same kind of tenderness I had in my heart for my mum. It was entirely unexpected—a depth of empathy I hadn't known before, and on some distant level, perhaps love. How could I love a woman I had never met?

I felt protective of her. I wanted to reach back in time and help her, to stand with her, and to let her know that she was not alone. In years past, I had thought of what it might have been like for her to arrive at the hospital and go through the birthing experience all on her own. I had imagined that she felt shame, and perhaps she had carried that heavy burden throughout her entire life. But I had never put so many concepts together all at once. And until that moment, I had never felt such mercy.

I couldn't help but begin formulating an image of her that resembled the women rescued through the work of A21. How many times had I sat with them, listened to them, and grieved over their vulnerabilities as women who were lured with promises of a better present, a more hopeful future—if only they complied with some scheme that trapped them in a place they never intended to be.

"However you evaluate it, Christine, it was a very unequal relationship. He manipulated her. He took advantage of her."

Even though I had no way of knowing exactly what happened, the realization that my birth mother was just as at risk of being exploited as the women I help rescue was astounding. To wrap my mind around the idea that a woman so vulnerable gave birth to me—someone who fights against the very injustices this woman might have experienced—strengthened my purpose, my resolve. I couldn't reach back in time to help my birth mother, but I could remain faithful to the work of A21 and press on to help those still needing to be rescued.

YES—ALWAYS, TODAY, EVERY TIME YOU ASK

It was difficult to sort through all the emotions this one revelation evoked in me. Our relationships with our mothers are deeply complex, and mine was even more so. But I know where my help comes from, so, as is my custom, I turned to Jesus and his Word.[1] I needed his understanding, and I was confident he wanted to show me something.

Opening my Bible with my journal at hand, I began reading in John 5, where I had left off the day before:

Now there is in Jerusalem by the Sheep Gate a pool, in Aramaic called Bethesda, which has five roofed colonnades. In these lay a multitude of invalids—blind, lame, and paralyzed. One man was there who had been an invalid for thirty-eight years.

JOHN 5:2–5 ESV

For longer than Jesus had been alive, this man had lain under one of five porches surrounding the pool, where the poor, marginalized, sick, lame, and blind had gathered together in hopes of being the first one in the pool each time the water stirred—as legend said, the first one in would be healed. For thirty-eight years, this man had felt helpless to move or to change, destined to be at the mercy of everyone else.

> When Jesus saw him lying there and knew that he had already been there a long time, he said to him, "Do you want to be healed?"
>
> JOHN 5:6 ESV

The words jumped off the page at me. *Do you want to be healed?* I couldn't help but laugh aloud.

Jesus, you cannot be serious. I am *healed. I wrote a book called* Unashamed. *How much more could there possibly be? We've dissected every part of my being, every chamber of my heart, and put it out there for the whole world to read. I just wanted to explore more about my birth mother, not be turned inside out again.*

But the words continued to resonate in my heart: *Do you want to be healed?*

I had been here before. Enough times to know that there would be greater fruitfulness on the other side, great reward that would be exceedingly abundantly beyond what I could ask or think, just as he promises.[2] Enough times to know the way up is always down; the way out is always in. Enough times to know that he always works deeper in me before working more broadly through me, when he's preparing to impact more people.

Yes, Lord, I want to be healed. Always. Today. And every time you ask me in the future.

193

I knew this wouldn't be the last time he asked me, because there is always more—more healing, more wholeness, more intimacy with Jesus and more effectiveness for Jesus. There is always more transformation, more sanctification, and more freedom. Sometimes, embracing this "more" means going deep and cutting some things out, much like I shared in *Unashamed*. Other times, embracing more is akin to examining scar tissue or finding a bruise that needs tending, like it was for me in this season. But no matter the depth of our wounds, God's promise to us stands: "He heals the brokenhearted and binds up their wounds" (Psalm 147:3).

Every time Jesus has invited me into more healing, it has been unexpected. No matter how many times his invitation has come, no matter how many times I have taught about it, I can still get caught off guard. I can feel just like the man lying by the pool called Bethesda, surprised by an unexpected question. When Jesus met him, Jesus didn't help him move to the edge of the pool or give him money for food like we might expect. No, Jesus asked a question that went straight to the heart: "Do you want to be healed?"

Now, I have to pause and laugh at Jesus's poor pastoral care skills. Every church has a pastor who visits the sick in the hospital, and I'm sure that if he/she made a habit of asking, "Do you want to be healed?" a reassignment would be just over the horizon. You can't be the pastoral care leader and have zero bedside manner. I'm sure the training manual for hospital visitation clearly indicates how to approach the sick, and I seriously doubt that Jesus's blunt question with an insultingly obvious answer is on the list of suggested conversation starters.

But, as always, Jesus had a purpose. Just as he had a purpose when he used the grief I felt for my mum to lead me to tender places in my heart for my birth mother. He was digging deeper, actually asking the afflicted man far more: *Do you really want things to change? Are you willing to take on all the responsibilities that will become a regular part of your life if I heal you?*

Jesus wasn't just asking the man if he wanted to be healed physically, but if he wanted to be healed completely. He wasn't asking him a one-time question, but a lifelong one. Jesus knows it's so easy for us to grow accustomed to our limitations—to be defined by them, to make allowances for them—and not really want to pay the price of change. He knows how easy it is for us to settle for where we are and to live a smaller life than what he's called us to.

When he asked me, *Do you want to be healed?* he was asking me to go beyond where I had been healed before—beyond all the rejection and abandonment I had been healed from and had detailed in *Unashamed*. He was asking me to go with him to another level.

Isn't that what he does with all of us?

When we cry out wanting to be married, doesn't it stand to reason that his response might be an unexpected question: *Are you ready for the vulnerability and transparency of being in a relationship?*

Or when we pray for new friends, might he ask: *Are you willing to risk and invest your time and your heart . . . without any guarantees?*

We cry out to him, wanting to move forward, but how would we answer if he asked us: *Do you want to let go of the past once and for all, including forgiving all the people who have wounded you? Are you willing to do the work of uncovering bitterness and uprooting it altogether? Are you willing to give up trying to control every facet of your life? And make more room for me?*

I know that saying yes to Jesus's unexpected questions might be hard, but saying yes is always the way forward. It's so easy to settle for where we are, to get comfortable with things as they are. It's so easy to get stuck.

Stuck.

That's the condition the man's answer to Jesus's question exposed. When asked by Jesus if he wanted to be healed, the man didn't say, "Yes! Finally! Are you kidding me? Of course, I do. Who wouldn't want to be healed?" He said, "Sir, I have no one to put me into the pool when the water is stirred up, and while I am going another steps down before me" (John 5:7 ESV). Do you see what he did there? Go back and read it again. When Jesus offered him freedom, the man focused on his limitations. He was so consumed by his problem that he couldn't embrace the miraculous possibility literally staring him right in the face.

When Jesus poses his unexpected question to us, we have a choice to make. We can focus on our limitations and problems, or embrace the miraculous possibility he offers us. We can run away saying a loud no, or run forward proclaiming a loud yes. When Jesus asked if I wanted to be healed, I could have dismissed it or offered an excuse. I could have busied myself, compartmentalized my emotions, and refused to "go there" in my heart, justifying my decision in a multitude of ways. But, unlike the man by the pool, I knew the value of healing. I knew that there would be more freedom waiting for me on the other side. I knew that my healing wasn't just about me—that there were people to reach beyond myself. So I said yes.

It is easy to focus on our limitations instead of our freedom, to be consumed with our "pool problem" instead of with the hope of Jesus's healing. It's easy to pass up his invitation, to be so focused on everything that's wrong that we are incapable of seeing the miracle Jesus offers us. It's easier to keep our eyes fixed on our limitations:

- I didn't go to the right school.
- I don't know how to do anything else.
- I don't have enough education.
- I'm trapped in this town.
- I didn't come from a wealthy family.
- I have no trade, no skills.
- I don't know where to start.

All that man had ever known was his infirmity. His pain and place of limitation were his comfort zone. Instead of saying an enthusiastic yes, he placed blame on others for his plight, and held onto his condition.

It's incredible, isn't it? But the truth is, we've all been there. We've all done that.

We've clutched the reasons why we can't fulfill our purpose.

We've held onto our anger or disappointment, unforgiveness or offense, bitterness or rejection, addiction or greed.

We've all found ways to adapt to our brokenness instead of risking the responsibilities of wholeness. It's much easier for us to post and hashtag about being wounded than it is to take the risk of being healed.

How many times have we stayed right where we were and blamed someone or something else for our misery? Our spouse or children? Our coworker or boss? How many times have we believed that being stuck wasn't our fault, and all the while, God was showing us the way out?

When the man dodged Jesus's direct question, Jesus simply

ignored his response and issued a command: "'Get up! Pick up your mat and walk.' At once the man was cured; he picked up his mat and walked" (John 5:8).

Think about this for a minute. If you've been lying on a mat for thirty-eight years, what does that mat represent to you? How would you feel if someone tried to take it from you? Can you imagine your life without it? That mat was the man's security, and perhaps the only source of comfort he had ever known. So when Jesus commanded the man to get up and pick up his mat, he wasn't just healing his body—he was challenging his sense of safety. He was also challenging the source of his identity as a helpless victim. That was what was behind Jesus's question from the beginning. Not just, *Do you want to be healed?* but *Are you willing to give up this old identity for a new one? Are you willing to give up your limitations for freedom? Your victimhood for victory? Your blaming for owning? Your disappointments and bitterness for grace and forgiveness?*

"Get up! Pick up your mat and walk."

When Jesus healed him, the man had been lying by a pool called Bethesda—a name that literally means "House of Mercy" in Hebrew, or "House of Grace" in Aramaic. When Jesus healed the man, he ministered to him both mercy and grace. When Jesus heals us, he extends to us the same mercy and grace, and he wants us to receive it with open arms. He wants to help us get to the place where—in every area of our lives and hearts—we come to realize what God has done *for* us is bigger than what others have done *to* us. Where what God has said about us is greater than what others have said about us or to us. *Do you want to be healed?* is a question that Jesus asks over and over again throughout our lives, and he always wants our answer to be, *Yes!*

ANOTHER UNEXPECTED INVITATION

I'm aware more than ever that nothing can change the events that got me on the mat in my life—that nothing can change how I was birthed by one woman and adopted by another. But I know mercy and grace are what got me up and walking, and mercy and grace are what have continued to open doors of destiny in my life.

When Jesus extended an invitation to me for more healing, he exposed mother wounds I didn't even know were there. In his great mercy and compassion, he wanted to help me. When I went back in time to explore more about my birth mother, I found another place in my heart where I was lying on the mat. And when I did, I said yes to Jesus, picked up my mat, and walked again.

I'm so glad it wasn't the first time he'd asked me if I wanted to be healed of something, and I'm certain it won't be the last. At this stage of my life, because I've walked through so much, and been healed of so much, it's more of an expected question than an unexpected one. And I want it. I want my next season in life—of marriage, motherhood, and ministry—to be even more fruitful than the last. I don't want to miss anything God has intended for me—and I know he doesn't want me to miss anything either.

Not long after I walked through this process, God did something very special for me. It felt like he just gave me the biggest smile, an unexpected gift that touched me so deeply. I opened my email to find an invitation to Mumbai, India. I was to be honored with the Mother Teresa Memorial Award for Social Justice on behalf of A21 for our work around the world rescuing slaves.

An award in the name of Mother Teresa. Of all people! If ever there were a mother figure in modern history to honor, it would be Mother Teresa. She was a nun who devoted her entire life to missionary work, who felt called to the poorest of the poor, who spent the most fruitful years of her ministry in the slums of Calcutta. She founded an order of nuns whose ministry reach eventually spread to manage orphanages, AIDS hospices, and charity centers worldwide—caring for refugees and the sick, those displaced by epidemics and famine, those who were the most vulnerable in every society. She was honored with a Nobel Peace Prize in 1979.[3]

I was overwhelmed at the goodness of God. The poignancy of God. The timing of God. Nothing is accidental.

As I typed my reply, I couldn't help but smile right back at God. I would say yes to this invitation just like I had always said yes to his, because saying yes is always the way forward, into more of our purpose, into more of our destiny.

Chapter Ten

WHEN THE UNEXPECTED EXCEEDS WHAT YOU IMAGINED

Pressing In and Pressing On

None of us knows what the next change is going to be,
what unexpected opportunity is just around
the corner, waiting a few months or a few
years to change all the tenor of our lives.
—KATHLEEN NORRIS

Scrolling through the day's news reports on my phone, I froze when I saw the pictures of a rescue worker holding the lifeless body of three-year-old Alan Kurdi[1] on the beach in Greece. *He was just a child. Some mother's baby.*

As I read the story, my heart wrenched. Somewhere in the choppy seas while crossing from Turkey to Greece, Alan's father, Abdullah, had tried to hold onto his wife and two sons after the boat they were in capsized, but the waves had ripped them from his grip. Like so many other Syrians who had made the same journey, the three of them had all drowned. When

Alan's body washed ashore, the world began to take notice. And so did I.

Desperate to know exactly where on the shore of Greece this happened, I checked the map and scanned more news reports, but I came back to the first story about Alan. As I reread the article and stared at the picture, all I could think about was his father—a man desperate to save his family from the terror of war, now grieving even more than the loss of his home, community, and homeland. Now he had truly lost everything. He'd lost his family.

As I began to pray for him, I found myself sobbing. I had heard these same kinds of stories before. I had heard of brave men like Abdullah Kurdi when my parents, aunts, and uncles would share our family history. My grandparents had fled from Izmir, Turkey, for Greece, and then Egypt, in 1922, during the Greek genocide. There, in Alexandria, Egypt, a truly cosmopolitan city and the gateway to Europe, they worked to reestablish their lives and raise their family in peace.

In 1952, the nationalist generals overthrew King Farouk, and the Muslim Brotherhood became a powerful force. Christians became a persecuted minority, and my parents had to leave Egypt, just as their parents had to leave Turkey. Along with tens of thousands of other Greek families, they immigrated to Australia. I'm so grateful that I was born and raised in a nation that welcomed refugees and immigrants, and gave our family an opportunity to start again. My mum and dad always spoke with great gratitude and love for Australia.

Although I could in no way truly understand the plight of these Syrian refugees, I could understand that these were people created in the image of God, longing for safety and security for their families. Longing for an opportunity to have a hope and a future. Longing for peace and stability. Just like me. Just like you. They had dreams for freedom that had turned into a nightmare. Unfathomable pain. Loss. Heartache. Grief. Despair.

Still crying and still staring at Alan's picture, I could sense God wanted to show me far more than this child. He was the one who had captured the world's attention, but what about the thousands upon thousands of others who went unnoticed? The ones especially vulnerable to being trafficked? After all, no one looks for refugees, so no one notices if they go missing. I had to do something. We had to do something. God had led us to position our first A21 office in Greece, and there had to be something we could do. Nick and I called Phil, the director of our A21 operations.

OASIS OF LIFE

In late 2015, Phil accompanied nine of our team members to the northern border of Greece, and what they found was astounding. Thousands of people—later estimated to be as many as fifteen thousand per day—were sleeping in an open field with no shelter and no safety. The only thing that marked the separation between Greece and the neighboring country was a set of train tracks and a couple lines of trees. On the Greek side of the border was a field of potatoes, and on the other side a vineyard—everything on both sides was parched, dusty, and desolate.

Our team had brought along a Syrian friend named Omar in hopes he could translate if needed. When the young man stepped out of the car, he immediately saw his brother—a brother whom he'd not seen or talked to in more than a year. As Omar yelled out his brother's name and ran to him, our team watched their reunion in awe. Torn apart and displaced when their hometown was ravaged by ISIS troops, they had no idea if they would ever see each other again. It was so evident from the start that God was in this with us.

As Phil, his wife Nina, Omar, and others from our team walked into the sea of people, they talked with them, trying to determine what would be the best way to help. They met lawyers, engineers, designers, artists, teachers, even a famous volleyball star. But in this farmer's field, they were just families—fathers, mothers, and children all running for their lives. As our team waded farther in, walking among groups of families, they observed that there was only one water faucet for thousands of people. It was in that unexpected moment that they realized the most powerful way to help these people would be to provide water. Providing water would not only meet their most basic human necessity, but also give A21 an avenue to interact with them, educating them about the dangers of human trafficking so they could keep their families safe on the road ahead.

The next day, Phil and team members Tony and Kali met with officials and began devising a plan. They secured more than five hundred tons of gravel to be delivered to a site near the border to support semi-permanent structures. The gravel provided a foundation for the work of A21 and other international aid organizations, including the Red Cross, Doctors Without Borders, and United Nations High Commissioner for Refugees (UNHCR), to set up huge tents and toilets.

Within ten days, through the ingenious work of engineers, and the incredible global supporters of A21, we began building water stations out of shipping containers—oases of life. When you have nothing, water is everything. Inside each container was a row of twenty sinks flowing with fresh water for refugees to wash themselves. To refill water bottles. To rinse out clothes. To experience some semblance of normalcy in a world turned upside down. And because initially the camps also had no electricity, we installed solar panels on top of the water stations to provide light at night and improve safety.

A MOTHER'S LOVE

In the middle of the greatest migration of people since World War II, in an unexpected global crisis of epic proportions, we had the power to make a difference in people's daily lives and help save them from potentially being trafficked. As refugees, they were vulnerable. If they were looking for work, they would be prime targets. The day after Alan's body washed ashore, police detained four suspected traffickers on a Turkish beach—a beach where thousands of refugees stepped into boats hoping to make it to Greece's coastline.[2] The threat to their safety was as real on this shore as it was in the turbulent seas.

Continuing to get updates from Phil, I knew that I had to go. It wasn't enough to simply watch their plight on TV, read about in a newsfeed, or hear their stories second or thirdhand. I wanted to be with them. I wanted to look into their eyes and speak with them—even if through an interpreter. I wanted to hear their stories and let them know there were people in the world who cared about their safety and welfare. Just as I had wished I could for my own birth mother in her vulnerability all those years ago, I wanted to stand with them, to let them know that they were not alone, to let them know that they were loved and valued.

Getting there as soon as the arrangements could be made, I first spent a day being briefed and prepared by our team in Thessaloniki. The following day, we set out in the late afternoon to visit the first camp. During the hour-long drive, we saw buses headed in the opposite direction. Phil explained that each day around 5 p.m., buses were loaded with as many as seventy people at a time. Authorities were transporting refugees to other locations where they could catch trains for the next leg of their journeys—all in their efforts to reach other countries in Europe, such as Germany, Sweden, and the Netherlands, wherever they would be accepted. Listening to him, I thought back to my own family. They too had fled on foot, by bus, by train and boat. They too had no idea where they would settle, but knew that it had to be better than the war and certain death they had left behind.

When we arrived, and as I stepped out of the car, I was very attuned to the gravity of this moment. Looking around, taking in as much as I could, I was immediately aware that it was the dead of winter and bitterly cold—that I had warm clothing, a hat, and gloves to protect me, but they did not. Seeing the tents, I couldn't help but think that I had a warm bed back home, and they had neither a bed nor a home. I had eaten a hot meal before I came, and they had missed all too many. I had come from dry ground, and they had traversed a frigid sea. I had a sense of security about my life, and they had left all that behind. I had freedom, and they had none. I knew where I would be going when I left, but they had no certainty about their next destination.

Seeing a group of volunteers handing out coats a few yards

away, I felt compelled to join them. I wanted to help in any way I could. The line, filled with fathers and mothers and their children, appeared to go on forever into the fading sunlight of the camp. *How many thousands of people are here?* As I was handing out coats, I heard a woman shouting on the other side of the fence that had been built around the camp. Turning, I realized she was yelling directly at me.

I didn't understand her Arabic, but I didn't have to in order to know what she was saying. I glanced at her two children and understood she was begging for me to give them coats. I used my best gestures to communicate that she needed to get in line, but she kept pleading. She wasn't giving up. *Unyielding. Determined. Pressing in past a crowd. Seeking what she desperately needed.* She reminded me of a woman who behaved much the same way when she came to Jesus for healing, and she did not stop until she touched the hem of his garment and was made whole.[3]

I felt caught between helping those who had waited patiently in line and yielding to her persistent demands. Looking at her directly, trying to decide what to do, I saw such desperation. She was probably two thousand miles from home, wherever that was back in Syria. She was alone—unusual for a Syrian woman—and like everyone else standing in line, she had risked her life to get to this point. Based on the stories our A21 team had heard from many of the refugees, she had probably spent days not knowing how she would feed her children, separated from family and community—her husband killed or missing. And, although I obviously didn't know her, I recognized her strength. It was the same strength that caused parents like Adrian and Jayne to fight for Fraser. The same strength that rises in us to overcome fear and embrace the unexpected with courageous faith. The same strength that enables us to persist against all odds, when we know we are called by God to act.

Suddenly, unexpectedly, the mother instinct in me empathized with the fierceness of her love. If I had been her, I would have been screaming loudly too, demanding just as much. I would have abandoned all manners of the civilization that I'd left behind as well. All the protocol of an established society and modern culture. I would have done whatever it took to survive and protect my children.

Feeling the cold through my own jacket, I quickly threw her two coats over the fence. Her eyes thanked me. I was overcome, and it was all I could do to not bawl my eyes out. But I choked back my tears out of respect. I was determined to stand strong with them.

That night—more than any other in the eight years since starting A21—I was grateful we had never given up and quit, even though I couldn't count the number of times I did not know . . .

If we would have the funds to keep rescuing people.

If we could keep paying the price it took to go into the darkness with the light.

If we could continue to endure the intense spiritual warfare we encountered.

If our family could continue to handle the pressures of traveling so much.

If I had what it took to keep leading a global anti-trafficking organization.

If I could endure the disappointment of people leaving the work who had promised to stay.

If I simply had it in me to keep going—for a multitude of reasons.

Fighting for justice can sound so romantic, but that kind of idealism is found only in novels. The long-term work of justice is bloody, messy, painful, exhausting, and, at times, downright disappointing.

But then you have a moment like this one—when you look into the eyes of a desperate mother thanking you for something as essential as a coat on a brutally cold day—and all the labor, all the toil, all the sacrifice, all the pain, all the hardship, all the disappointment, all the commitment, all the perseverance, all of the fight suddenly become worth it. Every single time. For every single one. Because, truthfully, it's always about the one. It always was and always will be. I was thankful I was right where I wanted to be, right where I felt God had called me to be.

WHO AM I?

More than a decade ago, when Nick and I first began researching the possibility of establishing an anti-trafficking organization, we were given a terminal prognosis: *impossible.*

The feasibility study from the consultants we'd hired used that word ten times in their report. *Ten times.* And opening an office in Thessaloniki? It was the worst location we could pick, they said. They cited several legitimate reasons, including a lack of laws against human trafficking, corruption, and economics.

But Thessaloniki was the best European location to fight global slavery because it was in the middle of the biggest gateway illegal migrants followed into Europe. Traffickers knew this route, as it had been used for thousands of years for slave trade. Even the apostle Paul encountered this heinous crime when he intersected with a slave girl on his way to a place of prayer in the city of Philippi, a mere two-hour car ride northeast of Thessaloniki.⁴ Just as in biblical times, modern-day traffickers had been preying on innocent victims there for years—luring them from impoverished nations with promises of work and hope for a better life.

Why would God tell me to do something so impossible?

It would have been so easy to stop right then. No one would have blamed us—especially if they'd read the report we did. But impossible is where God starts, and miracles are what God does. So we began where God starts. It wasn't easy getting our vision up and running, but by the grace of God we moved forward.

Many times in the process of meeting with officials and working through obstacles, I felt so unqualified. *Who was I to tackle something like this?* I had no idea how to run an anti-human trafficking organization. I had no training in how to rescue slaves. I didn't know the right people. I didn't have all the resources I needed. I had no idea where God was leading us. I had to walk by faith and not by sight. I had to trust in the Lord with all my heart and lean not on my own understanding. I was the mother of two children under four at the time, living on the other side of the world, already working a full-time job. I was not looking to do something else.

But then, there was this unexpected call from God. He does love to surprise us. I knew I was unqualified, but I was willing, and I knew I had to draw my confidence from the Word. There seemed to be a precedent in the Bible for God using people who considered themselves unqualified, insecure, and incapable. When they obeyed and did what he called them to do, it ensured that he received all the glory. Isn't that who

Moses was? He was on the backside of the desert tending sheep when God asked him to go back to his homeland—Egypt—to rescue three million Hebrew slaves and lead them to freedom.

I was passing through a small regional airport when God drew my attention to posters of missing women and children. Especially to a child named Sophia—just like my own Sophia. God was asking me to help find tens of millions of slaves scattered around the world and to rescue them. How could I not, at the very least, experience the same emotions as Moses, to raise the same three objections he did, ones familiar to us all?

Who am I? Moses felt insecure and so did I—and I pointed this out to God just as emphatically as Moses did.[5] But God told Moses that who he was didn't matter as much as who was with him. My insecurities didn't matter any more than Moses's insecurities did. What mattered was who was with me, who had called me. *God* had called me. I chose to trust in that truth every time I met with an official or an expert who had so much more knowledge than I did. I had to believe that *greater is he who is in me,* and *I can do all things through Christ who gives me strength.*[6] Just as in everything else, I had to rely on God's Word.

Who are you, God? Moses didn't yet know God as intimately as he would come to know him in the years ahead.[7] So it is with all of us when we begin to fulfill our purpose. Every new initiative God has called me to start has deepened my relationship with him—whether it was when I was driving around the backside of Australia teaching youth, forming Equip & Empower Ministries, establishing A21, initiating Propel, writing books, or launching a TV program. As I have chosen to press in, to keep growing through every season of my life, I have discovered deeper truths about who God is.

I continue to learn that his Spirit in me is enough in every situation, and that I can do all things through Christ that strengthens me.[8] It is never about who I am not, but rather, it is always about who he is in me.

I'm not eloquent of speech.[9] Although I had experience teaching the Bible and sharing my testimony, I had never spoken to people about human trafficking. In fact, I felt entirely inadequate to do so. I did not know the right terms to use, nor did I have the right education to qualify me for this type of work. How could someone as unqualified as me speak to experts in law enforcement, government, community groups, or the media about slavery? I felt like Moses going before Pharaoh, the highest person in the land, to tell him to let the slaves go. And God assured me just as he assured Moses: *I made you, and I will help you. I will teach you what to say.*[10]

My guess is that you can relate to every one of Moses's fears and questions just as I did. How many times in a typical day do we let our fears lead us away from our purpose?

I'm not good enough.

I'm not talented enough.

I'm not educated enough.

I'm not resourced enough.

What if I fail?

Moses even went as far as to tell God to pick someone else.[11] God didn't send someone else in Moses's place, but he did send his brother Aaron to go with him and support him. With God's power, Moses overcame his initial fears and went to Egypt to confront Pharaoh—a king whom three million Israelites greatly feared.

By the grace of God, Nick and I moved forward too, knowing that any success we would have in helping to abolish slavery everywhere forever would have nothing to do with us or our limitations but everything to do with God's great power at work in us. What would be impossible for us would be possible for God, because with God all things are possible, and nothing is impossible.

THE COURAGE TO TRUST

Trusting God, Moses (and Aaron) went to Egypt, where Aaron told the Hebrew elders God's plan for Moses to confront Pharaoh and lead the Hebrew slaves to freedom. Together, they went to face Pharaoh—for the first of eleven times.

Their first visit was to ask if the Hebrew people could attend a festival in the wilderness—and Pharaoh of course said no. He had three million working slaves and had no intention of giving up his captive labor force, even for a brief festival. This is where God stepped in to give Pharaoh an object lesson.

> Aaron threw his staff down in front of Pharaoh and his officials, and it became a snake. Pharaoh then summoned wise men and sorcerers, and the Egyptian magicians also did the same things by their secret arts: Each one threw down his staff and it became a snake. But Aaron's staff swallowed up their staffs. Yet Pharaoh's heart became hard and he would not listen to them, as the LORD had said.
>
> EXODUS 7:10–13

Can you imagine being in Moses's shoes? He finally agreed to this assignment to go before the most powerful man in the land, trusted God to show up, and then *wham*! Pharaoh's magicians showed off a power that was seemingly equal to God's. How could that happen? And then things grew worse.

Pharaoh's heart hardened, just as God had said it would, and he ordered the Israelites to keep making bricks—but now with no straw, a substance critical for brick-making. It seemed the only thing Moses's obedience had succeeded in doing was to intensify the suffering of the people he was trying to free. Needless to say, the Israelites themselves were none too happy with Moses.

Over the next ten visits, Moses appealed to Pharaoh to reverse his decision. With each visit, Moses had to continue to set aside his fears as he faced the most powerful man in the land. And each time Pharaoh's heart hardened, God struck the land with a plague. With every effort Moses made, things went from bad to worse.

And yet, Moses persisted. When Moses confronted Pharaoh, he walked in faith—not fear—because, "By faith he left Egypt, not fearing the king's anger; he persevered because he saw him who is invisible" (Hebrews 11:27). Confronting fear never ends, but being controlled by it can end. I know I've said this before, but I can't say it enough.

Often, when things get worse before they get better, harder before easier, darker before lighter, we doubt. We doubt God. We doubt his calling. We doubt his faithfulness. We give up. *I guess he didn't open that door. I guess he didn't call me. I guess this isn't his will.* When did God say that it would be easy? When did he say it would be effortless? Here are a few things I have learned over and over and over again while following God:

Closed doors do not mean that God is not opening a way.

Increased cost does not mean that God is not calling.

The presence of a battle does not mean the absence of God in the war.

Trials don't mean we are out of the will of God. In fact, they often mean we are precisely in the center of God's will—right where we're supposed to be, doing exactly what we're supposed to be doing. Fighting the good fight of faith. Standing. Believing. Because he is working in all things for our good.[12]

As Nick and I and our team in Greece kept taking steps of faith, we often ran into unexpected roadblocks. It felt like we were constantly being rerouted, something I find to be a common experience in the Christian life. When we say yes to God—to the dreams and ideas he places in our hearts—the roads are often winding, uphill, uncharted, and full of potholes. They frequently require unexpected detours, the kind that don't show up on any map. And sometimes it seems like it takes much longer to get there than we ever expected. So it was when we launched A21.

Many times, it would have made much more sense to give up, but God was at work positioning us and preparing us. And eight years later, as the global refugee crisis unfolded—a historic event with a once-in-a-lifetime opportunity to help people—God showed us just how faithful he is, especially when we don't give up.

When Moses answered God's call, he was consumed by insecurity and fear of a powerful enemy king. But by the time he led the children out of Egypt, he no longer feared the king's anger or what the king might do to him.[13] He was unafraid and full of confidence because his trust was in God. He chose to reject the report that decreed it was impossible, and to rely instead on the God for whom all things are possible.[14] That's why he never gave up—and why the Israelites were freed from their slavery and entered the Promised Land as free people.

UNEXPECTED DESTINY

When we face the kind of opposition Moses did, giving up too soon is always an option, but it's never the answer if God has placed something in your heart—if he's given you a promise, if you know something is his will. It takes courage to keep believing and moving forward, especially when your present looks nothing like your promise. Especially when the journey is nothing like you expected. That's when you have to hold onto *other* promises from his Word to keep yourself holding on in faith. Promises such as, "He who began a good work in you will carry it on to completion until the day of Christ Jesus" (Philippians 1:6).

If we stay the course—if we press in and press on—and not let fear cause us to give up too soon, then God will complete the work he began in us, accomplishing through us everything he desires. That dream. That plan. That idea. Even if it's saving millions of slaves around the world.

The night I gave that mother those two coats, more than a million others like her had risked walking from Syria, Iraq, and Iran through Turkey, paying for passage across the Aegean Sea in overloaded inflatable dinghies that were designed for thirty to thirty-five, but sometimes held as many as fifty or sixty men, women, and children.[15] If they made it through the frigid waters, they spilled out onto the beaches dehydrated, cold, sick, and sometimes dead.

One man whom our team befriended had survived when the boat he was on hit rocks and sank. As the boat was deflating, he looked at all the children crowded in the middle of the boat—all his nieces and nephews and cousins—and he knew he could only save one. He painfully saved his younger sister.

Like him, this mother begging me for coats had survived, but the cost was greater than I could comprehend.

I've never stopped wondering, *Where did that mother and her children go?* The news broadcasts for months continued to show images of people walking along roadways, across open fields, stopped at borders, detained for days, lining up to board buses. European leaders weren't prepared. Greece wasn't prepared. Thousands were walking across their northern border on their way toward any other European nation extending a hand of support. Really, anywhere safe. And they kept coming.

Their landing site was within an hour's drive from our offices, so the refugee crisis was on our doorstep. More than one million potential victims of human trafficking were being put in the most vulnerable position imaginable—just within our reach.

It was an unexpected tragedy, an incomprehensible global event, that compelled us to respond. In fact, multiple humanitarian organizations were. *But not everyone was allowed to respond.* The Greek government would let only "established" agencies help.

An unexpected twist.

We were established.

Because we had been working in Greece since 2008, we were considered qualified to help—and now we were facing the unexpected opportunity to save thousands of lives. The result of our faith didn't look like the blueprint we first imagined. *It was better!*

After seeing the impact that first water container had, we built and deployed fifteen more to Greek islands and other points of entry. People around the world gave generously and provided hope to so many who tragically found themselves on an unexpected journey to a new and different life. Painted white, these water containers featured large A21 lettering on their sides, and maps that indicated, "You are here." There were also warning messages about the dangers of human trafficking and hotline numbers to call if help was needed.

We created play areas for children and hosted family movie night screenings—whatever we could do to create a new normal and bring moments of laughter in the midst of so much uncertainty. On each camp visit, I loved sitting with the children, playing with them, trying to give them a taste of the childhood they'd left behind. Many of them hadn't smiled in so long, but they laughed as we played games with them.

To protect them and their families, we passed out flyers in multiple languages warning of human traffickers and their ploys. We also handed out children's comic books that illustrated the dangers of trafficking for kids in refugee camps with a story they could understand. As we educated families and trained aid workers on how to spot victims, reports flooded the hotlines, resulting in rescue for many victims of human trafficking. Every person who was kept safe through prevention or restored through our care was a precious life God allowed our team to reach. And every person was someone we didn't realize would be on the other side of our obedience so many years before when we first said yes to starting A21.

That evening as we drove back to Thessaloniki, I was overwhelmed by how hard and long our journey actually had been. Eight years had gone by since God had drawn my attention to the flyers of missing girls on an airport wall—eight years since I felt God urging me to do *something*. And because I did, we were doing far more than I had ever imagined.

Unexpected. Unplanned. Unfathomable. Difficult. Destiny. All because we didn't give up too soon.

GOD'S PROMISES DON'T EXPIRE

Sometimes it seems far more logical to give up than to keep having faith for something to happen. The dream or promise God has placed in your heart probably isn't logical. You may not have the resources. You may not know much about the mission. You may not even know where to begin.

Or your dream may be more personal. You want to see someone you love saved or healed. Whatever the dream or the promise, God keeps his promises—and whether or not it happens as we expect really doesn't matter.

Very little in my life has ever happened the way I thought it would—but God's plans have prevailed because I've never stopped believing in him and following what he has wanted me to do. I've learned over and over that he often does unexpected things in unexpected ways in unexpected places using unexpected people.

People like you and me.

For Nick and me, starting an organization that covered everything from rescue to restoration was not logical. No one was doing that then. But that didn't matter. God seems to rarely ask us to do something in which we have expertise. He wants us to rely on him, trust him, and stay connected to him—for as long as it takes. Whatever God has placed in our hearts to believe, to long for, to plan, to build, is never something to give up on.

So, what has God placed in your heart to do? What has he called you to do that you have yet to start?

There will always be opportunities to falter, to slow down, to give up. But there is an assignment carved out for you, and God wants you to fulfill it.

God has certainly not forgotten what it is. If he said it, he will do it. If he tells you to do something, he will help you accomplish it. It may take what *feels* like a lifetime, but *he will do it*. And the results will most likely be very unexpected. And by unexpected, I mean wildly better than you could hope or imagine.

A couple of months after my trip to Greece, our A21 office there received an urgent call from the National Human Trafficking Hotline. A group of seventy-seven men and women were being exploited by traffickers. Someone in their group remembered the flyer we'd passed out while they were traveling through one of the camps and reached out to a volunteer we'd trained on one of the first islands where refugees stop.

Every single one of them was rescued. Every. Single. One. All because we didn't give up too soon. All because we kept pressing in and pressing on.

EPILOGUE

Nearly all the best things that came to me in life
have been unexpected, unplanned by me.
—CARL SANDBURG

Since the day those seventy-seven trafficking victims were identified and rescued, God has continued to do the unexpected through the work of A21. He has continued to do above and beyond what we could ever have asked or imagined. We've seen survivors come into our care weekly—and sometimes even daily. We've witnessed a legal battle that carried on for years suddenly end with a trafficker sentenced to twenty years in prison. We've seen A21 expand into one of the worst human trafficking regions in the world—Southeast Asia. And not only did it happen, but it also unfolded in Thailand with a coalition made up of A21, the Royal Thai Government, the Federal Bureau of Investigation, and the U.S. Department of Homeland Security. Only eleven years ago, the experts had said all of this would be impossible. Not hard. Not challenging. Not highly unlikely. *Impossible.*

Impossible is where God starts. In whatever he's called us to do—in whatever purpose he wants us to fulfill—he wants us to move forward in faith believing him and looking to him . . .

So he can fulfill the promises he's given us.

So he can express his supernatural power in our lives.

So he can receive all the glory.

God wants to do the impossible in our lives. He did it in biblical times, and nothing has changed since then—not who he is, not what he does, not the way he does it.

Our job is to keep believing that God is good, God does good, and God is working all things together for our good and for his glory.[1] We must keep believing he still is working on our behalf—ordering our steps, opening doors, healing our hearts, working miracles, regardless of how we feel or the obstacles we face.

Every time God has called me to start something new, I've never felt like I had anything I needed. And yet, I always found that I had everything I needed—because I had faith. Not faith in myself. Not faith in others. Not faith in a system. Not faith in an idea. I had *the* faith that comes from having Jesus living inside of me. *In him* is everything I need—every spiritual blessing—including faith itself:[2]

In him, I have my life and light (John 1:4).

In him, I have everlasting life (John 4:14).

In him, I am complete (Colossians 2:10).

In him, I live and move and have my being (Acts 17:28).

In him, I am redeemed (Ephesians 1:7).

In him, I have power (Ephesians 3:20).

I know I have access to all that he is and all that he provides because he lives in me. And I know that if he asks me to do something unexpected, he's already gone before me.

Jesus came to give us life and life more abundantly—and that includes the adventure of the unexpected.[3] When we face the unexpected, God is looking for us to respond in faith.

Faith in him. Real faith. Living faith. Faith that stands on his character. Faith that believes Jesus is who he said he is and that he will do what he said he will do.

Faith is all he really wants of us. Faith to trust him with the amazing, overwhelming, unexpected adventure he's planned for us. Even when we feel intimidated, unqualified, or under resourced. Even when it's uphill, painful, or full of struggle. Even when we doubt what we're doing is his will. (Yes, I have those thoughts too.)

I have learned what God's Word says . . .

That faith in God pleases God,[4] and that without faith, it is impossible to please God. *I want to please God.*

That faith is the substance of things hoped for, the evidence of things not seen.[5] *I want to believe God for all he wants to do.*

That faith in God moves mountains.[6] *I want to see mountains moved for his name, for his glory.*

Faith holds such unexpected power—the power we need to live our everyday lives, to fulfill our purpose. Without question, it's faith in God that gets us to our destiny. Always.

Faith in God is how we keep our hearts and minds fixed on where we're going. It's how we overcome the impossible and experience the supernatural—just as every biblical hero who ran this race before us did:

- Abraham, who left the known for the unknown (Hebrews 11:8)
- Sarah, who conceived despite her age (Genesis 21:2)
- Noah, who built an ark with the storm yet unseen (Genesis 6:14)
- Moses, who led the people out of Egypt (Exodus 6:26)
- Caleb, who trusted God wholeheartedly (Numbers 14:24)

- Joshua, who led the people to conquer Jericho (Joshua 5–6)
- Rahab, who risked her life to help God's spies (Joshua 2)
- Deborah, the judge who dispensed wisdom for more than thirty years (Judges 4)
- David, who defeated Goliath against all odds (1 Samuel 17)
- Esther, who risked her life to save the Jews in the Persian empire (Esther 5)
- Daniel, who feared God more than the king (Daniel 3)
- Shadrach, Meshach, and Abednego, who endured the flames (Daniel 3)
- Mary, who said yes to being the mother of Jesus (Luke 1:38)
- The man at the pool of Bethesda, who picked up his mat and walked (John 5:1–18)
- The woman with the issue of blood, who dared to touch the hem of Jesus's garment (Luke 8:43–48)
- Bartimaeus, who received his sight and then followed Jesus (Mark 10:46–52)
- Peter, who stepped out of the boat (Matthew 14:29)
- Philip, who shared the message of Jesus with an Ethiopian leader (Acts 8:26–40)
- Paul, who traveled the world to preach the gospel (Acts 11–28)

God isn't asking us to do anything he hasn't demonstrated for us in his Word, that he hasn't equipped us to be able to do, that he isn't going to walk alongside us to achieve.

There's no doubt God has called us to a purpose on this earth. We are his workmanship created for good works in Christ.[7] He has prepared many things for us to do here. We are citizens of another kingdom, and yet living in this very real and troubled world.[8] Wherever we find ourselves, whatever our sphere of influence, it is our mandate and our great privilege to bring a piece of heaven to this earth.

The unexpected adventure ahead of us is sure to have twists and turns that we didn't see coming, where the odds will stack up against us, but that's when God will have us right where he wants us. Perfectly positioned to walk in faith; believing for signs, wonders, and miracles; expecting him to make the impossible more than possible.

Faith is the path out of every obstacle and impossibility.

But we have to look up high to God, from whence our help comes from—instead of at our circumstances—so we won't succumb to fear.[9] I have heard the pounding footsteps of fear in hot pursuit of me with every step I've ever taken. But I have kept moving forward, believing that the same God who brought me this far will take me all the way to my destiny.

God is calling us to focus all our attention on him—our hearts, our minds, our eyes, and even our mouths. When I was diagnosed with cancer, I spoke only what the Word said about my healing. I didn't give voice to the fear and doubt that taunted me. When Adrian and Jayne fought for Fraser's life, they didn't give voice to the fear that taunted them. No, they chose a life of both/and—of moving forward in faith, despite the fear. God cares about how and why we say what we say—and he wants us speaking faith as we move *through* where we are to where he is leading us. He wants us to boldly declare that God will come through for us, even when we don't know how he is going to do it. He wants us trusting him wholeheartedly.

I was an unnamed, unwanted, adopted, abused girl from one of the lowest-income neighborhoods in Sydney, and somehow in his grace and mercy and goodness, God has redeemed my life, cleaned it up, and used me for his glory. At every juncture in my journey, it has never mattered what was happening in the world at the time, politically, morally, socially, or any other way. It has never mattered that there was chaos around me. It has never mattered if I had the team or the resources. It never mattered that I was a work in progress. All that mattered was that I was trusting him. That I was putting my faith in him, moving forward in faith, wholeheartedly believing that his every Word is true. That he who promised really is faithful.[10]

Isn't that what he did for everyone who so bravely shared their stories on the pages of this book? Adrian and Jayne. Amanda and LoriAnn. Kylie and Laura. He has led all of us out of fear, out of unforgiveness, out of hopelessness, out of loneliness, despair, and disappointment—and into our potential, passion, purpose, and destiny.

I believe he is doing the same in you right now.

We all are called to the unexpected, and it will always take faith to see it through, but when we move forward by faith, God will always fight for us and do the miraculous. Let's recognize what God is doing for us, the doors he's opening for us, the steps he's ordering for us. Let's affirm his supernatural power at work in our lives. He will always make a way where there is no way—though it may not be what we expect. He will always honor our obedience. In everything God has called me to do, the miracles happened *after* I stepped out in faith—after I stepped out in obedience, trusting him.

I don't know what your purpose is, but I know you have one. I don't know what God has called you to do, but I know you have a destiny. And I know, at every juncture in your journey, you will find yourself in an impossible place with a decision to make—to shrink back in fear or to rise up in faith. One will keep you where you are, and one will deliver you to your future.

I believe after reading this book and allowing the message of its pages to permeate your life, you will choose faith. I believe you will courageously choose to leave fear behind, move forward in faith, and embrace every bit of the adventure God has planned for you.

A PRAYER OF TRUST

As you move forward embracing all the unexpected adventures God has for you, I invite you to pray the following prayer. Pray it in faith, boldly, courageously, and with a passionate love for Jesus. Pray it with a thankful heart for all he has placed inside of you and all he wants to do through you. As you do, know that I'm praying for you as well, and together, we will move forward in faith, giving him all the glory for the rest of our lives.

Love, Chris

Father, your Word says that we overcome not by might and not by power, but by your Spirit. So, I lean into you, believing that you are at work in the unexpected adventures in my life. I trust in your goodness, no matter my circumstance. I stand on the integrity of your character, especially when I face the impossible. You are good. You do good. And you are working in all things for my good. You came to set me free, so I believe you for freedom, hope, healing, rescue, and deliverance. I choose to believe that impossible is where you start. Miracles are what you do. I believe in the name of Jesus for signs and wonders and miracles in my life. I believe for the supernatural in every area of my life—in my marriage and parenting, in my ministry and career, in my friendships and community. God, you are greater than anything I face. I refuse to fix my eyes on the obstacle and enemy, but instead elevate my gaze to you. I will speak your words of life and truth, agreeing with you alone, believing you are who you said you are and will do what you said you will do. You are faithful. You will come through. That's who you are. That's what you do. By your grace, I will live by faith. By faith, I believe you will fulfill your purpose for my life—that I will reach the destiny you planned for me all along—and I will give you all the glory in everything I do as we travel there together. In Jesus's name I pray, amen.

ACKNOWLEDGMENTS

There are so many people involved in bringing a project like this to completion. I certainly could never have done it alone. I'm so grateful for my village, for everyone who has brought their gifts and talents, their wisdom and brilliance, to the table with such full hearts.

To my husband, Nick, and to our girls, Catherine and Sophia: You are God's most precious gifts to me, my greatest loves, and the joy of my life. Your love and support during the long and arduous writing process means the world to me.

To Adrian and Jayne, Amanda-Paige, LoriAnn, Kylie, and Laura: Thank you for allowing me to share your stories. Your vulnerability and generosity will help so many.

To our A21, Propel, Zoe Church, and Equip & Empower teams, volunteers, partners, and supporters: Changing the world with you one life at a time is the greatest privilege and honor of my life. Thank you to all the team members who agreed to be interviewed, who confirmed facts and stories. Your contribution was invaluable.

To Elizabeth Prestwood: You are the most amazing collaborative writer on planet earth. Without you, this book would not be what it is. You are a gift. Let's keep doing this.

To Kristen Morse and Rebekah Layton: Thank you for

reading more drafts of this book than anyone ever should. Your insights, suggestions, and comments helped more than you can ever know. I love you both so dearly.

To the Zondervan team: It is an honor to work with you. Your commitment and dedication have been invaluable to the outcome of this book. Thank you for believing in this project from the beginning—and for being willing to go with another "Un" title. Thank you, Sandra Vander Zicht, for your encouragement from the onset. Thank you, David Morris, for your support and belief in yet another book. Thank you, Tom Dean, Alicia Kasen, and Robin Barnett along with the entire incredible marketing team, for your innovative and creative ideas to expand the reach of *Unexpected*.

To Joyce Meyer: Your unconditional love has been one of the greatest unexpected blessings of my life. You have loved me and nurtured me as if I were your own. I wouldn't be who I am if I had not met you. I wouldn't be where I am if you had not believed in me, supported me, encouraged me, accepted me, corrected me, and guided me. Words could never express my gratitude to you or for you. I will forever love you.

To my Savior, Jesus Christ: Thank you for leading me through the unexpected and healing me so I could trust you through it all. I can't wait for what's next!

To you: I am so grateful to you for reading this book and trusting me with the message God placed in my heart. Thank you for pursuing your purpose with anticipation for all the unexpected ahead!

NOTES

Chapter 1: When the Unexpected Interrupts

1. Romans 8:28.
2. James 1:17.
3. 1 Timothy 6:12.
4. John 16:33.
5. Colossians 3:15.

Chapter 2: When the Unexpected Brings Fear

1. Romans 8:15.
2. 1 John 4:4.
3. Proverbs 15:24.
4. 1 John 4:8, 18.
5. 1 Peter 5:7.
6. Psalm 121:4.
7. Matthew 6:9–13.
8. Daniel 3:27.
9. Galatians 5:22–23.
10. Luke 22:42.

Chapter 3: When the Unexpected Disappoints

1. Luke 24:17.
2. Luke 24:17.
3. Luke 24:18.
4. Luke 24:19.

5. Luke 24:31.
6. Luke 24:33.

Chapter 4: When the Unexpected Betrays

1. *Unashamed* by Christine Caine, chapter 8, "He Healed My Mind," pp. 133–47.
2. Deuteronomy 31:16; Hebrews 13:5.
3. Proverbs 18:24.
4. Romans 8:28.
5. Acts 8–10.
6. Luke 23:34.

Chapter 5: When the Unexpected Disillusions

1. James 4:8.
2. John 14:6.
3. Matthew 5:4; 2 Corinthians 1:3–5.
4. http://www.insight.org/resources/bible/the-minor-prophets/Zechariah.
5. Hebrews 10:35.
6. Jeremiah 29:11.
7. Matthew 9:24.
8. Isaiah 61:3; Psalm 103.
9. Proverbs 13:12.
10. Ephesians 3:20–21.

Chapter 6: When the Unexpected Disheartens

1. Numbers 33.
2. Joshua 5:6.
3. *New American Standard Exhaustive Concordance of the Bible* (Nashville: Holman Bible Publishers, 1981), 446.
4. Numbers 14:30.
5. Numbers 13:27.
6. Exodus 13; Numbers 11; Numbers 20.
7. Hebrews 11:1.
8. 1 Peter 5:7.

Chapter 7: When the Unexpected Requires Risk

1. Psalm 37:23.
2. Numbers 13–14.
3. Genesis 15.
4. James 2:23.
5. http://lists.ibiblio.org/pipermail/b-hebrew/2008-September/036236.html.
6. 1 Samuel 17:4.
7. 1 Samuel 17:50.
8. Psalm 121:1–3.
9. 2 Chronicles 20:15.
10. http://www.prb.org/Publications/Articles/2002/JustHowManyBabyBoomersAreThere.aspx; https://www.census.gov/newsroom/press-releases/2015/cb15-113.html.

Chapter 8: When the Unexpected Is Incremental

1. Isaiah 6:8.
2. Zechariah 4:10.
3. 2 Corinthians 5:7.
4. Isaiah 49:16.

Chapter 9: When the Unexpected Calls for Change

1. Psalm 121:1.
2. Ephesians 3:20.
3. http://www.motherteresa.org/biography.html; https://www.nobelprize.org/nobel_prizes/peace/laureates/1979/press.html (Mother Teresa).

Chapter 10: When the Unexpected Exceeds What You Imagined

1. Alan's name was originally incorrectly reported as "Aylan" in news reports. https://www.wsj.com/articles/image-of-syrian-boy-washed-up-on-beach-hits-hard-1441282847; https://www.nytimes.com/2016/03/05/world/europe/syrians-sentenced-aylan-alan-kurdi.html.

2. http://www.independent.co.uk/news/world/europe/aylan-kurdi
   -s-story-how-a-small-syrian-child-came-to-be-washed-up-on-a
   -beach-in-turkey-10484588.html.
3. Matthew 9:20–22.
4. Acts 16:16–18.
5. Exodus 3:11–12.
6. 1 John 4:4; Philippians 4:13.
7. Exodus 3:12–22.
8. Philippians 4:13.
9. Exodus 4:10–12.
10. Exodus 4:12.
11. Exodus 4:13–17.
12. 1 Timothy 6:12; Ephesians 6:13; Romans 8:28.
13. Hebrews 11:27.
14. Mark 9:23.
15. https://www.pri.org/stories/2015-10-09/beautiful-turkish-tourist
    -town-now-home-boats-stuffed-refugees-and-migrants.

Epilogue

1. Romans 8:28.
2. Ephesians 1:3.
3. John 10:10.
4. Hebrews 11:6.
5. Hebrews 11:1.
6. Mark 11:23.
7. Ephesians 2:10.
8. Philippians 3:20.
9. Psalm 121:2.
10. Hebrews 10:23.

Dive deeper into *Unexpected* with your church or group!

In the *Unexpected* five-session video Bible study, bestselling author Christine Caine shows that while most of us have been trained to fear the unexpected and want everything to be "under control," God wants us to anticipate the unexpected with a faith-filled perspective rooted in trust. He has never been taken by surprise with the unexpected, and he wants us to move from a life filled fear, control, worry, anxiety, panic, and feeling stuck to one full of hope, walking in faith, and trusting in him. We can step into the destiny and adventure that God has for us by dealing with pain barriers, managing disappointment, strengthening our hearts, building our faith, and expanding our lives.

Sessions include:
1. Move into the Unexpected
2. Strengthen Your Heart
3. Choose Your Destiny
4. Press Through to Breakthrough
5. Expect the Unexpected

Unashamed

Drop the Baggage, Pick up Your Freedom, Fulfill Your Destiny

Christine Caine

Shame can take on many forms. It hides in the shadows of the most successful, confident and high-achieving woman who struggles with balancing her work and children, as well as in the heart of the broken, abused and downtrodden woman who has been told that she will never amount to anything. Shame hides in plain sight and can hold us back in ways we do not realize. But Christine Caine wants readers to know something: we can all be free.

"I know. I've been there," writes Christine. "I was schooled in shame. It has been my constant companion from my very earliest memories. I see shame everywhere I look in the world, including in the church. It creeps from heart to heart, growing in shadowy places, feeding on itself so that those struggling with it are too shamed to seek help from shame itself."

In *Unashamed*, Christine reveals the often-hidden consequences of shame—in her own life and the lives of so many Christian women—and invites you to join her in moving from a shame-filled to a shame-free life.

In her passionate and candid style, Christine leads you into God's Word where you will see for yourself how to believe that God is bigger than your mistakes, your inadequacies, your past, and your limitations. He is more powerful than anything you've done and stronger than anything ever done to you. You can deal with your yesterday today, so that you can move on to what God has in store for you tomorrow—a powerful purpose and destiny he wants you to fulfill.

DVD curriculum and study guide also available

Unstoppable

Now with Study Guide

Running the Race You Were Born To Win

Christine Caine

Each of us has a race to run in life. But this is a different kind of race. It's more than a competition, greater than a sporting event. It's a race with eternal implications—a sprint to destiny.

But many times in our race, we're burdened and intimidated by life's challenges along the way. The task seems too tough, the path too perilous, the race too rigorous.

What if you knew the outcome of the race before it began? What if victory was promised before the starting gun ever sounded? This truth would change the way you live your life—revolutionize the way you run your race.

Slow out of the blocks? *It's okay. Don't give up!*

Trip and fall in the first turn? *Doesn't matter. The race isn't over!*

Disheartened by an unexpected obstacle? *Keep going. You can make it!*

In *Unstoppable*, bestselling author, global evangelist, and human-trafficking activist Christine Caine enthralls us with true stories and eternal principles that inspire us to run the race of our lives, receiving the baton of faith in sync with our team, the body of Christ.

Your race is now. This is your moment. When you run with God in his divine relay, you can't lose. You're running the race you were born to win.

Available in stores and online!

Unshakeable

365 Devotions for Finding Unwavering Strength in God's Word

Christine Caine

God is bigger than your current story. Bigger than fear or shame or that voice in your head that whispers that you are not enough, too broken, or too flawed. Join him in a closer relationship—one rooted in truth and *Unshakeable*. In this yearlong daily devotional, bestselling author, speaker and activist Christine Caine encourages you to find confidence to live as the person God created you to be.

Everything in our world that can be shaken will be shaken. And yet, the Bible assures us it doesn't matter what happens politically, morally, socially, or economically in the world around us if we have Christ in us—if we have the kingdom of God within us—because his kingdom is *Unshakeable*.

Through inspiring personal stories and powerful Scriptures, Christine Caine will equip you to live boldly and courageously, fully trusting our faithful God. She will inspire you how to activate living your life on mission. Unstoppable. Undaunted. Unashamed. *Unshakeable*.

"All of creation will be shaken and removed, so that only unshakable things will remain."—Hebrews 12:27 NLT

Available in stores and online!